POKING TH
IN THE EYE

Realstew and
The Butterfly Effect

Empowering Communities One
Person at a Time

Kay Urlich
with Paddy Delaney

RealStew: is a Social Co-operative committed to the philosophy of giving the lion's share of all revenue back to its members and the community. RealStew is also a technology company, an online hub designed to revolutionize the way the world communicates and interacts. RealStew has integrated all the different ways we connect – chat, email, social media, user groups, websites and blogs on one platform housed in a single internet browser.

Holacracy: is a well-tested theory which allows for different more humanitarian principles to be used in an organization, rather than adopting traditional, hierarchical structures. This radically changes how an organization is structured, how decisions are made and how power is distributed.

Energy Fields: a means by which the energy structure of any entity can be measured. Four energy fields and their traits are a fundamental structure within the universe which applies to all living things.

"Have a healthy disregard for the impossible"
Paddy Delaney

*"Do we need to understand right now, whether
economics as we understand it, is fit for modern
economic life?"*
Christopher Houghton Budd

Acknowledgments

Many thanks to Paddy Delaney, Christopher Houghton Budd
and Steve Smith for generously sharing information,
knowledge and support.
Special thanks to Jenny Hunt for tireless patience and sage
advice while editing this book.
There are those who remain anonymous and
unacknowledged, to whom I am deeply indebted for their
time, support and encouragement.

ISBN 978-0-473-29388-8

Contents

INTRODUCTION by Paddy Delaney

"Action without vision is only passing time, vision without action is merely day dreaming, but vision with action can change the world." Nelson Mandela

Yes, of course we set out to change the world and *Poking the Bull in the Eye* is a project I have been working on with Kay Urlich as part of the change process.

This Bull represents not only Bull Markets and the legalized fraud which distorts action in the investment market, but also the fraudulent culture which operates in established banking practices. Bull also calls into question the controlling and all pervasive nature of global corporations, along with their huge power and wealth which they use to dominate and manipulate the lives of countless millions of people.

While I am not against these institutions as such I am absolutely against their practices. Practices which are long established, hierarchical in nature and which make sure that as much of the profits as possible are funneled upwards to a minority of the already over-wealthy.

I am not against being rich, but am against using wealth to gain an unfair advantage in all aspects of life. In the same way, I am not against capitalism as a construct, but I am against the corruption which is rife in capitalism.

The victims of Bull actions are countless, world-wide and on-going. They are responsible for the newly poor, the further impoverishment of the already poor and many other hard working people and communities whose lives have been negatively affected. Bullish tactics and actions have decimated whole populations as well as natural resources. Land, mineral extraction, forests, oceans and lakes have been stripped and destroyed in the name of profit and greed.

We have all seen this happening around us for decades and felt powerless to change it. Wealth and power in the hands of a few who have the resources to protect and increase their assets have created the enormous seemingly bridgeless divide between those who have and those who have not.

Why was this able to happen in the first place and why does it continue to happen?

The lack of sharing and humanitarian principles which have been so well cultivated in these monstrous entities makes them impenetrable to the average person. They generate fear and mistrust because few viable alternatives exist and those that do are subject to crushing competition.

Kay Urlich's discovery and research of Energy Fields clearly discloses the underlying energy structure in all entities and because of these insights I cannot help but see the extreme energy imbalance within these huge financial, political and religious institutions. The world we have now is weighted heavily in what Kay defines as hierarchical 'ManWorld' traits which have created an empire of power; a collective, separate and superior place. In fact, by doing this, 'ManWorld' has achieved the worst-case scenario predicted by George Orwell's 1984 nightmare. Total Power.

Humanitarian qualities of caring for the vulnerable, compassion, protection and mercy, some of the female energy traits which have been excluded from all systems, without exception for eons. Contribution from 'WomanWorld' is essential to bring balance, openness, inspiration, and acknowledgement that the sharing of wealth and resources is a form of nurturing and valuing every person and every person's contribution to their community.

Around the world, women are expected to align with the dominant male values as dictated by whatever their culture is. This expectation is of course no different or less troubling for men, who simply for the sake of having a job, must frequently align with an indifferent, free-market capitalist society.

Realstew and The Structure of Energy Fields are both new ventures which have grown out of existing philosophies and practices. They have come into being now as a response to the over-riding need for change if we and the planet are to survive. What may seem like small actions made now can have remarkably big consequences later and certainly they can and will influence the future for humanity.

Applying Energy Field patterns to societies, cultures or communities back though time shows us exactly how and why we reached the current unworkable power structures we all have to answer to today. Basically, it was the decision to control our own food supply that propelled us into the modern world. Systems and structures were established and these began to dominate the more organic lifestyles that had functioned well for all members of those groups for eons because they valued and honored all life while sharing Earth's resources.

These hunter gatherer societies made way for 'civilizing' systems, and an imbalance of power began to affect the working of personal energy structures. Men and women had shared equal status and certainly, women's ability to coax life from the soil was recognized. However, male and female equality shifted as power moved into the hands of a few and soon women became objects, something to be controlled rather than co-operated with.

From small beginnings in a garage in the Waitakere ranges, our big dreams grew into enormous dreams and these dreams have continued to expand so that RealStew now has a Global presence. We are a Global community and our founding principle of being a Social Co-operative committed to giving the lion's share of all revenue back to its members and the community is firmly established.

To say that for me, this process is enjoyable would be an understatement. Challenges are many and constant and that's what I love. Every challenge overcome is a step forward and for RealStew to now be established in London, a global city and an international financial centre, places us exactly where we need to be. Real change never starts at the centre, rather it filters in from outside and if it is strong enough, it reaches the centre as RealStew has done.

Collaborating with Kay Urlich as we 'Poke the Bull in the Eye' is also a statement about not only gaining a deeper understanding through Energy Fields of the raging bull we have to deal with, it is also saying, "Watch it bull, you won't always have it your own way."

I thoroughly recommend this book to all RealStew members and to everyone else who wants to see and participate in change in their life-time.

CHAPTER ONE

What has the Sale of Coffee got to do with Prison Systems?

"Any customer can have a car painted any color that he wants so long as it is black." Henry Ford

Energy fields and their traits are a fundamental structure within the universe and they apply to all living things. Every person, every business, community, culture, village and society live within a 'structure of energy and form', and all people succumb to their culture, through one form or another. Furthermore, when any business, culture or financial system is placed against this 'Energy Field Structure', its human traits or lack of them, financial abundance or lack of it, as we shall see with Free Trade and Bull Markets are immediately evident; the structure of energy field traits brings a consciousness of knowledge which is transparent and leaves no hiding place for treachery. The Structure of Energy Fields is a system to assist in both personal and professional life, while at the same time it allows you to track a company's progress, just as we are doing throughout this book with RealStew.

For example, how far does your money go these days: buying food, keeping up the mortgage or rent payments? How safe is your job or business? How do you feel about the present banking systems that are running one sided schemes which could be contributing to your financial downfall?

It is a well-known fact that free trade monopolies are moving throughout the world and that multinational companies are negatively impacting on every small business owner and worker on the planet. Do you feel that the blood sweat and tears it takes to find work, keep a job, run a business, pay for basics such as housing, food and clothing, and education for your children now takes considerably more effort to achieve than it did twenty years ago? Or even worse, because of the present financial crisis, that all the effort you made to achieve security for your family turned out to be a big waste of time.

In view of the combined wisdom of experts around the world, one would wonder why a global financial crisis even exists; why are millions of people in dire financial need? New laws in Cyprus, which are insinuating their way into Greece and Spain, appear to give governments the right to remove a percentage of savings from personal bank accounts. Additionally, in a Free Trade environment, why are over seventy million youth now unemployed and millions more about to lose their jobs?

"There was a reason why our founding fathers were wary of monopolies - because they knew that too much power and influence in too few hands was not conducive to liberty and freedom..." Britain's *Independent* reported recently.

The paper goes on to say that "three mega-multinationals now control more than 40 percent of global coffee sales. Cocoa growers now get only between 3.5 and 6 percent of the average retail price, while in the 1980s they earned about 18 percent... Take the case of Gerardo Arias Camacho, a 43-year-old coffee farmer from Costa Rica. He has been producing coffee since he was removed from school to help his father farm the commodity at the age of 10. Today, he works 13 hours a day to produce coffee from about five hectares (about 12.3 acres). Camacho, who is a board member of the first *Fairtrade*-certified co-op in Costa Rica, said this year he will likely struggle to make even a small profit from some of the coffee he produces and sells. "About 40 percent of our coffee is sold to multinationals, but the problem with the free market is that there is no minimum price," he told the paper. "Last year, I got $2.20 per pound of coffee; this year it's about $1.40. This is really bad for us, as the cost of producing is about $1.60." Interestingly, about 500 million small farmers produce some 70 percent of the world's food and women are at the forefront of this alarming statistic, producing 60 to 80 percent of the food in developing countries and acting as the primary producers. Source *NaturalNews.com*

Equally alarming is the influx of young people who are thrown like rubbish into USA prisons system. Why does the USA incarcerate a higher portion of its population, compared to the smaller numbers in other countries?

- USA have 760 prisoners per 100,000 citizens
- Japan: 63 inmates per 100,000 citizens
- Mexico: 208 inmates per 100,000 citizens
- Britain: 153 inmate per 100,000 citizens

What you might ask has the world trade in coffee got to do with the US prison system expanding at a rate far greater than the rest of the world, again, increasing the chasm that exists between the employed (the majority of whom do not receive a living wage) and the unemployed, the rich and the poor? A chasm which as it grows wider creates ever greater divisions in society, at the same time amplifying global and social unrest, creating what are clearly insupportable levels of inequality in societies. Rising crime rates among young people and inadequate physical nourishment, along with poor living conditions, are the inevitable result.

Consequently, along with the rise of Free Trade Markets there is a wretched growth in the number of people experiencing mental health problems and depression, which has put greater stress on all social and justice systems that are now dealing with the swelling numbers of homeless, financially desperate and displaced people. You would again need to ask — what can be done about it? Or more to the point, do we need to change the way we view success; do we first of all need to adjust our perspective to discover the root cause of why such ruthless discrepancies persist and find new ways to solve ongoing global problems by exploring new financial paradigms?

CHAPTER TWO

**How do you explain a New Business Model designed
exclusively *for* you, which is not all *about* you?**

*"In all chaos there is a cosmos, in all disorder there is a
secret order"*
Carl Gustav Jung

How good would it have been to have had shares and
input into Facebook at its conception, to buy into
financial and social history for a few dollars or cents a
share? Imagine too, if the massive income that Mark
Zuckerberg receives was shared amongst its many
members. Instead of one person receiving such massive
profit, it was shared amongst all members of the
Facebook community so that they all received a
percentage of the financial transactions generated by
the network around them.

In keeping with this theory a new global network
has come into being; one that not only has all the tools
of Facebook but is designed to give the lion's share of its
revenue back to the community. RealStew has also
developed a leading edge communications platform
which is an innovative new business and technology

concept that shares company profits with all its members.

As with Wikipedia and Mozilla Firefox this company is fully owned by participants and can never be taken over by wealthy individuals, big banks or large corporations. It is a business venture to capture the imagination of the individual, offering so much more in return for their effort and commitment. Its vision is much wider and more beneficial than other social and communication companies with a focus on transparency, sharing and individual empowerment. On more intangible levels, it is a concept designed to activate the inspiration and consciousness of humanity

Do you remember, being a child when you were innocent and idealistic and life was simple? Did you wish you had lots of money so you could buy the things you wanted? Were you kind and generous and did you spend time talking and listening to old people? Did you want to send your dinner to China because your mother said little children were starving there? Were you ready to rush out in a storm to save wet and frightened animals?

If you remember the excitement you felt at the thought of sharing your skills, no matter how simple they were, it could be that you are still connected to the innocent, uncluttered dreams of childhood, of a less complicated world. A time when you understood clearly the answers to problems that plagued not only your little mind, but the minds of much of mankind because then it didn't seem hard to solve the problems of lack you saw in the world. Lack of compassion and kindness, lack of food and shelter were not perceived as problems because you *knew* what to do about them.

Sadly as time passes it seems for many that the optimism, magnanimity and self-belief of childhood fades as conditioning from their culture takes over, often attached to the fear of failure even when there is plenty: plenty of food, plenty of education, and yet in a world dominated by an unequal distribution of wealth and resources it can still seem as if there is not enough.

The boldness of childhood, the dreams and goodwill of youth are edged towards the back of the mind; childhood awareness is recalled as mere hallucinations which come and go like colorful mirages as innocence is enveloped in the world of adulthood and survival. Where for some children life is so brutal, that there is little time to rest and no place for peace, let alone the luxury to dream of a better world; there is little choice but to strive for survival in harsh competitive environments.

Visions of creating a kinder more interconnected world fade as the fear of financial failure impacts harshly on the young, particularly those who get caught up in the panic of food shortages, or who face the consequences of floods, famine or earthquakes. Depending on prevailing political situations, many are subjected to the frequent and brutal realities of war. These are disastrous global events which can take hold of mass consciousness then swiftly expand into the terror that comes with ignorance of the unknown.

For instance proponents of the Mayan Calendar, many of whom forecast the end of the world in 2012, got it wrong; the time came and went and the world did not end. Yet at the same time the world as we knew it changed in both subtle and profound ways. While poverty, disasters and war are still rampant there has been a vast shift in human consciousness. Frequent reports from TV news and the internet indicate that those who continue to operate within old dominant dictatorships of greed and survival of the fittest are being challenged and pushed aside.

Change within the global mind, means the old fear tactics used to control populations are not working as they once did. The time of world domination and the coveting of power by one section of the population, or one individual over others by those who have risen to the top of a hierarchical self-perpetuating cycle are being forced to look at alternative methods of governing. Holacracy, a global trend which offers diverse and more humanitarian principles is gaining in popularity.

Holocratic systems have much in common with the social awareness principles of *Rudolph Steiner's Threefold Social Order* as described by Stephen E. Usher Ph.D.

Steiner's theory as developed between 1917 and 1922 states: "The core concept recognizes three domains of human social activity: economic, legal, and cultural. Steiner maintained that the health of human society depended on an adult population that understood the characteristics of each domain and could thereby organize society so that each domain enjoyed independence and autonomy." In fact, Steiner held that it would be socially destructive if one of the three domains attempted to dominate the others. Economic life should be centered around transforming what nature provides in the mineral, plant and animal kingdoms into commodities that *meet human needs.*"

CHAPTER THREE

Distributed Authority

"I have not failed, I have just found 10,000 ways that do not work." Thomas Edison

Holacracy is a theory based on the principle that an individual can achieve maximum levels of personal freedom and autonomy while cooperating and interconnecting with the goals of others. It depends on power not being held by a group of dominating individuals or corporations.

Under a holacratic system, each individual, without control from someone further up the chain, can set and is encouraged to set his or her priorities. In this way, they are empowered to control their own work and achieve their own goals. Empowerment brings responsibility and a share of authority which is a basic concept of Holacracy, i.e. that authority does not issue from one source but is distributed among many.

Similar in theory to the food we eat where nutrients are not siphoned off for the benefit of only one organ, life-force spreads throughout the body to sustain the health of the whole system.

Based on this same principle there are four energy fields, of varying levels, that flow through the body, mind and spirit, some of which receive little or none of the nourishment they need to maintain a healthy, balanced state. In the same way, the unequal distribution of global finance has resulted in massive wealth for a small portion of the population and levels of poverty from severe to hopeless abject despair for many millions more. Moreover, in energy field terms, there is little evidence of any improvement in the present economy, or solutions that would alleviate these problems by maintaining peace and prosperity, through the wellbeing of an interconnected global community.

The Structure of Energy Fields show how the life-force of the planet has gone to feed and nourish only one organ, mainly the lower left brain functions. By sectioning off this one area, financial power has favored very few human traits and in this, it has elevated those chosen from the whole interconnecting system. This has served to promote and maintain greed and control based financial theories that separate much of the global population from corporate profit.

In Energy Field terms it means that poverty has exploded around the globe and this stems, as illustration 1 indicates, from the actions of this one area of human consciousness. It is an area that promotes a strictly dominant and materialist view of success; profit is its purpose. It is of no consequence that the financial wealth of a few comes at the cost of a large portion of the population's emotional, mental and spiritual wellbeing.

Active
Masculine
Logical
Competitive
Independent
Closed
Hierarchical

Illustration 1

It begets harsh rationalist ideologies such as those espoused by free trade advocate Milton Friedman, who in a raft of policies which have spread globally, leave little place in the international community to ease personal financial worries, or promote workplace interconnection.

And the question we must ask now is, how can a theory such as holocracy be activated to nourish the more intangible aspects of a global society that is locked into a rationalist financial point of view? How does an awakening society conduct such a massive shift in financial consciousness?

Don't laugh, but try to imagine Free Trade theorists deciding that instead of soaking up as much global financial wealth as they can for themselves, they change to a more sharing mode of operation. I know it's crazy, but imagine if the present Wall Street's corporate overlords began distributing a large percentage of corporate America's profit amongst all members of the community, in a system that developed financial interaction with others all over the globe.

Then people like Gerardo, instead of being squashed out of business by the present Free Trade system, could expand his family's livelihood and their *Fairtrade*-certified co-op in Costa Rica, and sell their product into similar local and overseas markets; to connect with those people who foresee a better world. To connect with others who are seeking change and who are eager to participate in and benefit from the support they would receive by sharing a greater financial vision.

Not only would Gerardo and his family gain a great lifestyle by receiving more profit from their own business, they would also receive company income from corporate business activities. In so doing, it would mean instead of the present fragmented distribution of wealth, life-force in the form of money, would flow more easily, feeding equally into all four energy fields of the community and country, benefitting and nourishing everyone instead of fattening one already over-fed field.

It is nice to dream, but it is unlikely we will ever see such change from within the present Free Trade or Wall Street mindset. And it is at this point that The Structure of Energy Fields explains RealStew's main points of difference in global business: Instead of promoting another Wall Street corporate structure that soaks up all the profit and simply adds to the huge financial imbalance that now exists in global society, RealStew has created a system to nourish vast areas of untapped and unused human potential.

Innocence	Compassion
Curiosity	Protector
Inspiration	Divine Love
Mercy	Empathy
Active	Nurturing
Masculine	Feminine
Logical	Intuitive
Competitive	Passive
Independent	Interdependent
Closed	Transparent
Hierarchical	Inclusive

Illustration 2

By mobilizing multiple energy field traits such as transparency, empathy and mercy, to work in conjunction with those traits already in power, a new financial vision is born, a vision with the potential to create an opportunity for greater personal and global achievement.

RealStew holds a space to activate and transport the ideas and theories we have into reality. By feeding more than one area of the human financial environment, as its corporate wealth spreads, it aligns with new world consciousness to activate, nourish and expand wealth; by distributing corporate profit through a unified energy field system, it is doing what Wall Street will not do

A unified financial energy field structure allows for the reemergence of the more constructive and progressive actions between community and environment. In this way RealStew's financial business practices bring alive and spread higher human values throughout society where the wealth and power, formerly held by one quadrant of energy, can now flow to all parts of the community and benefit each member of society; it is a system that allows more humane actions to flourish.

RealStew is revitalizing a damaged global market place, as it supports in business the concepts of interdependence, inclusiveness and transparency which feed increasing amounts of compassion and curiosity, in other words, life-force back into the very communities that have for decades struggled to sustain Wall Street profit; those communities that for decades have been sucked dry by the overwhelming abuse of power, and unbridled greed of a free financial market.

Then, in this freer more awakened environment, when we are curious about the world we live in, we can find fulfillment in doing what we are good at, or aspire to do in an organization that values our service financially no matter how inconsequential the traits we use may appear, or have appeared in the past. In this way RealStew is structured to not only share massive global wealth more equitably, but to raise global consciousness.

CHAPTER FOUR

Purposeful Action

"Use your imagination not to scare yourself to death, but to inspire yourself to life."
Adele Brookman

RealStew was co-founded by visionaries Paddy and Mandy Delaney. With a healthy disregard for the impossible, they set about remodeling global financial systems and business markets to make them more user-friendly to the needs of people, rather than institutions. Paddy has instigated an equitable and sustainable financial system which reflects the present trends in technology while supporting not only the individual and their community, but the environment as well. The network which has been formed has the potential to create personal wealth for many while providing financial support to community and charitable concerns.

RealStew as a social co-operative supports the aspirations of dreamers and visionaries, welcoming new ideas as a major part of bringing into being a more balanced social and business environment, while sharing the organization's global profits in practical magnanimous ways. This is a commercial structure that like a balloon expands as each of us, our friends and business concerns engage within it and grow with it.

Change, in the form of holacracy, is occurring on many levels of consciousness; physically, emotionally, mentally and spiritually – real shifts are taking place in small communities and being cemented into society, then stabilized through evolving shared and secure global market places. You need only check this, or any company's progress against Illustration 2 of the energy field structure, to see if they are on track, or not.

The term holocracy has been replaced in the RealStew community as *The RealStew Way;* a way that is activating theory and bringing it into global action. By doing this, the new model of finance is promoting a form of democracy based on financial security thus showing that wealth is not just for a few at the top of the global financial mountain. A significant aspect of Democracy which RealStew aspires to is the personal power it bestows through financial wellbeing.

When the RealStew NZ Manager of Professional Support, Anita Harris was asked why she was so involved in this process, she said "I've never really had to dig too deep for the answer. My distaste for the greed that I see in the world, the way people use power to have control over others, things that are so ridiculously priced that the average person may never get ahead. I have a love for the way in which people working together can triumph over tremendous adversity and to be able to give the average person the tools to communicate in a way that for so long has been out of reach. Including the struggling small business and the successful business, now all can be on the same page. Through *The RealStew Way*, I am fortunate to be able to work with others who feel the same way."

Paddy and Mandy named RealStew after the elements that were key to their vision. Loyalty to the following principles became the foundation of the RealStew brand.

It was a humble beginning with a few people working from a garage in Auckland, New Zealand but it has grown quickly into a global enterprise. It only takes a small change made somewhere in an established system to create huge differences to outcomes at a later stage and in another place, as The Butterfly Effect states.

RealStew has now gone beyond the garage dreams, and its initial achievements which were sufficient for it to become accepted into the ICEHOUSE Executive in Residency Program on 18th February, 2013. This was a great mile-stone for RealStew and gave them access to mentoring and assistance to grow to the next level. The

Ice House is a NZ government sponsored incubator group focused on growing NZ businesses.

RealStew is an acronym for:

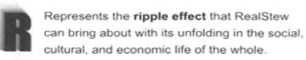 Represents the **ripple effect** that RealStew can bring about with its unfolding in the social, cultural, and economic life of the whole.

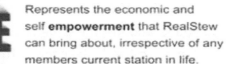 Represents the economic and self **empowerment** that RealStew can bring about, irrespective of any members current station in life.

 Represents the **abundance** that can unfold.

Represents the **life-changing** impact that the RealStew movement can bring about.

Represents the mantra of **sharing** that RealStew supports.

Represents the transparency of RealStew processes.

Represents the energy that will flow from Members working together.

Represents the economic, cultural, and social wealth that RealStew can generate in the world.

Contact with a visiting British Trade Attache indicated that the next most advantageous move for RealStew was to establish a base in Britain. Accordingly, Paddy, Mandy and family relocated to London in December, 2013. *RealStew Financial Services* will be launched from there and shares will be floated on the London Stock Exchange.

The potentially chaos creating vision of RealStew, its dream of a globally interactive and financially nourishing environment has only just begun: the flutter of a butterfly's wings in New Zealand has created an impending hurricane which is building force globally.

The Faculty of California describes chaos as it pertains to finance and mathematics. "Chaos is the intellectual achievement of man finally realizing the staggering complexity within the natural world and his ability to formalize it using mathematics and technology. Because a system's complexity typically resides well below the surface of ordinary experience, chaos, as a principle of scientific thought, could not arise without special tools and mathematical insight to probe these depths."

More than that, change is occurring as we activate a wider range of energy fields, allowing increasing human sensory and inspirational factors to take place. When human intelligence rises each one of us can experience more of our potential while accessing information that cannot be gained through normal, or traditional, education methods or human thought systems.

"Similarly," the Faculty of California continues "The development of the digital computer has made chaotic modeling and experimentation possible. Computer processing power allows for the simulation of complex systems such as meteorological phenomena. Computers are becoming increasingly adept at simulating the multitude of interactions that take place within a typical physical system. Because the brain is a highly complex system and can be described using *nonlinear* functions, the field of chaos is beginning to be adapted into fields such as psychology and education. Add to this a growing awareness of the vast and wonderful life around us, and the expansion of human intelligence traits, and you have a compelling recipe for the expansion of human consciousness...In effect, early and contemporary paradigms of scientific thought were unified in their preference for a system which favored only one state or one well-defined subset of states which have become the bench mark, or their 'norm', causing "any divergent behavior to be rejected as a negligible freak occurrence". In reality, the behavior of complex systems cannot be neatly described and accurately predicted.

We live in a chaotic world where anomalies (or other aspects of the system) can no longer be neglected or "averaged out", but must be embraced as vital occurrences that could drastically alter the future of a system."

CHAPTER FIVE

Energy Fields: A Structure of Intelligence

"It is a miracle that the curious survive formal education."
Albert Einstein

With thoughts of divergent behavior in mind we can think of the unused vital inspirational energies of the human energy fields where people were said to be crazy if they had thoughts, or dare I say visions, of life outside established scientific theory. Many believe that we use less than 10% of our brain power, and despite this speculation, the power of left brain linear thinking is still claimed by many to be the ultimate in human intelligence. Even if, as Illustration 1a demonstrates, there is growing evidence that most of humanity has been activating only limited aspects, of a wide ranging list of human possibilities.

Why and how has the idea of linear function of the brain been able to overcome all other energy field qualities and what does this actually mean for us? How do we find ways to use the phenomenal range of intelligence that is held within a whole and connected body, mind and spirit? Like the energy field graph, how do we discover, use and promote globally the amazing range of untapped human potential?

Human energy field systems are viewed differently dependent on your point of view, or on your perceptions of intelligence. The language may be different but Dr Robert Sternberg, the Dean of Arts and Science at Tufts University, Boston, views intelligence factors differently from the rationalist norm. His view is that, "the perception of intelligence factors has changed. Traditionally only one factor is measured for I.Q. tests, and that is analytical ability, which means humanity generally, is using limited aspects of whole brain theory". The reality is, we actually need to be measuring three, which Stenberg calls the Triarchic Theory of Intelligence.

- Analytical ability
- Creative ability
- Practical ability

By limiting students to the present analytical measurement of intelligence the education system doesn't work for the majority. It never did work well because by using only one part of our brain power traditional educational and business models, like old financial business systems, were drawn out and separated from a great pile of human energy traits; this then separated people from a wider range of values and qualities essential to humanitarian principles.

It follows then that many people have been stifled since birth from using their inherent intelligence and the natural structure of their individual energy field resources. This has served to block the development of childhood possibilities, and it is this hidden individual potential that we have yet to reveal, which will lead us to explore the untapped universal resources of creativity and knowledge where answers to the problems that presently plague mankind can be found.

The world is changing rapidly but how well does the rationalist mind keep up with the momentum? Is it time to reassess the wider situation, or more to the point are we awake enough to look at new options that are out there now? This means that for change to occur we must begin by opening ourselves to a greater life-force, one that is hidden within the subtle energy field aspects of human consciousness, those areas that are not so easy to measure; to those intangible fields that cannot be seen or understood through normal physical channels.

There is only one way to do this, and that is by stepping out of our comfort zones, or those paradigms we are so familiar with, to seek and explore new ways of doing things.

By looking at new business systems and seeing what they have to offer, we can then measure them within the energy field model to see if they hold space for change to occur. Change to the current momentum of business, by challenging old brain methods and functions of analysis and logic, and expand these limited traits to include other aspects of whole brain energy field structure. In this way, we can understand whether their actions differ from their theory.

Are they hierarchical and limited in content? Do they expand to include all people along with their dreams and visions? Do they increase their potential by raising the level of interdependent human endeavour? Can we expand our minds beyond the purely physical viewpoint and explore life through a unified energy field theory, to activate a greater range of human ideals?

CHAPTER SIX

Timing is Everything

"Without initiative, leaders are simply workers in leadership positions." Bo Bennett

Paddy Delaney learned at an early age how to achieve his goals. When his father offered one shilling pocket money Paddy hatched a clever plan. He told his father that rather than a shilling he would take any pennies in his father's pocket. Paddy was a chip off the old block and his father was a wise man. He always seemed to finish up giving Paddy a shilling in pennies. Paddy hatched plan 'B'… at the end of the day Paddy asked his father to exchange his twelve pennies for a shilling piece. The next day Paddy asked his father if he had any pennies!

Paddy wanted to win so badly but he was also a realist and dyslexic so reading was difficult and therefore he had to work a lot harder. Through this he became strong minded and strategic, understanding that luck came with hard work … and he wanted to be lucky! But he knew he would also have to be resourceful, imaginative and inventive if he was to win whatever prize he had set his heart on.

He later came to understand that sometimes you don't always receive what *you think* you want, because the universe has other ideas and takes over. As a senior high school student, he was heartbroken when after winning a competition and feeling that the world was now his oyster, the girl of his dreams ran off the guy who got second in the competition, in other words – he lost.

Paddy realized that many times in life, losing one prize may lead you to another which is much better in every way. 'Serendipity,' says Paddy.

After he and his first wife divorced, Paddy attended a dancing class with a friend. Mandy was the dance teacher and on meeting her, he vowed to his friend that Mandy would be his future wife. He enrolled in a rival dance school and took a crash course in Ballroom dancing. Upon asking for a lunch date he was at first declined. But in the end by a process of charm and persuasion, he got the date and he and Mandy married a few months later.

Those who have worked with Paddy to manifest the RealStew vision have become familiar with some of the inspirational phrases he uses. These have now become entrenched in the *The RealStew Way* ethic, known as 'Paddy-isms.'

- Have a healthy disregard for the impossible

- Listen to the gentle inner voice
- Act beyond duty
- Harmony through medium-ship not extremes: medium-ship is a way of taking a stand to find sustainable answers where anything is possible
- Step out of the box and do what you do for the right reasons
- Embrace change
- Find reasons to say yes
- Become a modern pioneer
- Anything is possible

As a follower of philosopher Rudolph Steiner, Paddy believes in Steiner's three fold system of social principles; the separation, yet interconnectedness and interdependence of the three spheres of collective human activity; cultural, political and financial. By achieving balance in those three spheres harmony will prevail in a community and everybody can achieve well in the game of life.

"Timing is everything" Paddy says "and the time is now". The time of injustice and inequality is coming to an end and now it is your chance to be part of, and help grow this wealth sharing, supportive enterprise."

In brief:

1.   **Firstly, says Paddy, let's talk finance.** We have the ability to improve the global financial

system, beginning with each one of us being empowered; where work is rewarded and the rise and fall of monetary value is due not only to the rise and fall of energy input but the connection of the 'peer-to-peer' network around you: where money is not created in a vacuum by printing empty currencies the value of which disappears in a flash as so many big companies have done. It is where everybody in the business instead of having to rely on phantom groups of self-invested and self-interested bankers, those people who invest their own time and money have access and ownership of their very own financial gateway. There is also the ability to buy and sell shares but because the majority of Real Stew shares are in a Trust, nobody can buy, sell or trade the RealStew Company. Like Wikipedia or Mozilla Firefox the public has ownership - there can be no big all-consuming power broker at the top and no corporate takeover.

2. **Secondly, cultural.** Steiner could never have imagined the power that we now have in our hands with the Internet, Social Media and Cloud Computing. We can literally build a global community that would have been unimaginable to Steiner, or even our grandparents!"

3.   **Thirdly, political.** RealStew is not, and has no ambition to be, a political party. But the ability to empower people and help them to be more informed makes *The RealStew Way* a force to be reckoned with!"

Global business is increasingly being controlled by Bull Markets and Wall Street, and the effects of this are featuring more and more prominently in our lives, so it is time to look at the aspirations of those who long to actively bring about a better world. Where significant and lasting change can be wrought through businesses such as the RealStew model: where, for those who dare to persevere, dreams and visions can become reality through pragmatic, innovative and interconnected socio-economic solutions. Where, as we shall see, rather than being a butterfly bowled over by the hurricane of free trade agreements, we are able to use the power of energy fields inherent in each of us to activate vigorous, connected communities. Through new eyes we can test the status of all business models, to see how they align, or not, within a *structure* that measures all physical, emotional, mental and spiritual human qualities.

The question is, "Are we better off with more Free Trade Agreements?" How can increasing social pressures and inequalities in society support the belief that we are better off with the policies that companies such as Monsanto and Corrections of America are creating as they continue schmoozing up to governments all over the world with the sole intent of expanding their own profit. They achieve this through a wider range of Bull markets which impact on communities which become powerless as they are subjected to the 'poverty virus'. This is marketing at its worst, causing social havoc throughout the world and creating global corruption which translates into personal problems for countless individuals. These large problems are dumped into our personal space, inflicting more stress and trauma onto each of us which then flows back into the community.

Take the following case of Monsanto's influence and tactics on one independent businessman.

Earlier this year, the Illinois Department of Agriculture allegedly stole and destroyed a beekeeper's hives and bees after inspectors claimed the hives had foulbrood, and that the beekeeper, Terrence Ingram, had failed to dispose of the hives as instructed. However, Ingram feels he could prove his hives did not suffer from the contagious disease, and that the Department acted without due process

- Mr. Ingram suspects the destruction of his bees may be more related to his research on Monsanto's

Roundup and his documented evidence that Roundup kills bees.

- One of the forerunning theories of colony collapse disorder (CCD) is that it's being caused by genetically engineered crops – either as a result of the crops themselves or the pesticides and herbicides applied on them, such as Monsanto's Roundup

- Ingram has studied the effects of Roundup on honeybees for the past 15 years, and believes he has acquired sufficient amounts of data to show that Roundup not only causes bee die-off, but may be the cause of CCD. Source Dr Mercola.com

Is this an isolated incident? I don't think so. Over time there have been more and more recorded incidents of corruption where large international companies gain power over small merchants globally: where those who dominate financially have gained government backing, and along with it greater authority and control of personal and community resources.

CHAPTER SEVEN

Social Collaboration vs Social Networking

"Tell me and I forget. Teach me and I remember. Involve me and I learn"

Benjamin Franklin

Without control of their own time and resources many people feel they are mice on a wheel driven into jobs they have little connection too. Turning up every day to do work that doesn't inspire them simply to eat and pay rent or the mortgage. Similar to the movie Ground Hog Day, every day is the same. And even with thoughts of a different life, a different way, there is no place to take these reflections and contemplation or, you could call them dreams, within the present business environment.

But there is light at the end of the tunnel with the rise of new companies such as RealStew which is set-up for individuality, and gaining ground because of its Social Collaboration based ethos which applies a group centric approach to securing an identified outcome, similar to crowd sourcing as it involves individuals working together toward a common goal.

- Collaboration among individuals is an appealing experience, because participation is 'a low investment, with the possibility of high return', which appeals to young entrepreneurs because of this notion.

Andrea Grover the founding director of Aurora Picture Show in Texas explains how she uses the collaborative through art "I am curious about the art analog to this growing phenomenon of mass volunteer cooperation, or crowdsourcing". Citing Jeff Howe who introduced the term in his June 2006 *Wired Magazine* article, "The Rise of Crowdsourcing" to describe a new form of corporate outsourcing to largely amateur pools of volunteer labor that "create content, and solve problems." Examples of online enterprises successfully built on crowdsourcing are abundant: EBay—which enlists users to stock a marketplace, consume from and police it; Amazon—which relies on users' product reviews to sell to like-minded shoppers; and the more recent Threadless—a company that prints and sells user-generated t-shirt designs based on popular vote. In his 2002 book *Smart Mobs*, Howard Rheingold called these consumer-driven ratings "reputation systems" and indicated that for the moment (barring radical changes to telecommunications law) consumers have the power to create what they consume".

Social Collaboration works when there is:

- Common purpose – collective goal – common ethos
- Mutual respect of all contributors and able to compromise
- Open communication channels
- Process and structure – rules of engagement (same side of road – same protocol)
- Resources – no one can live on 'love alone' – corporate model (donations)
- Resources are: Capitol / Time / Technology / Communication / knowledge

Where instead of the usual **Corporate Control** which employs and deploys, a **Social Collaborative** manages, empowers, and channels the energy of all people involved. RealStew takes this concept a step further, adding another dimension to Social Collaboration, whereby it *shares the company's profits* too.

CHAPTER EIGHT

A Fundamental Error in the Financial Reward System

"Corporation: An ingenious device for obtaining profit without individual responsibility." Ambrose Bierce

We have come to a point in time where not only are hundreds of millions of people suffering through unsustainable and struggling hierarchically based economies, but the majority are expected to lie down quietly as always and observe their own misery. Meanwhile, those in the strongest financial industries grab the largest pay-outs for themselves, leaving the average worker in lengthy discussions over who owns the bones; insidiously leading nations to war and destruction while fighting over the crumbs.

Meanwhile, as Americans bail out Wall Street – those receivers of Bull market income - and its banks which are the major Sub-Prime Bond creators and receivers of corporate welfare, the average worker whose job hasn't been outsourced, that is, those people who are lucky enough to have jobs, who haven't yet been turned into 'independent contractors', are falling far short of their expected income growth. Most are on the losing end of the financial spectrum within a system of fixed pricing that is not indicative of a truly free financial market based on the human value of technology or of the product or service in question; it is a market that keeps the majority dependent on the power of Wall Street problems and investors to the allure of high 'Bull positions.'

A Bull Position Means: A long position in a financial security, such as a stock in the stock market. A bull or long position seeks to profit from rising prices in certain securities. When prices rise, a bull position becomes profitable. If prices fall, the bull position is not profitable. A bull or long position is the most well-known type of position and is what is typically used in "buy and hold" investing. An alternative way to initiate a bull position can include buying call options.

A bull position is the opposite of a bear position. A bull position is a trade or investment that is initiated in the hopes that the instrument's price will rise and make a profit. A bull market occurs when prices are rising, and is characterized by investor optimism and confidence that prices will continue to rise. - Source: *Investropedia*

As we can see with Gerardo Arias Camacho, Terrence Ingram, and later with the free market prison system, Bull positions and prices are expected to keep rising despite their destruction of peoples' lives or welfare, or the lack of any value gained to the community they serve.

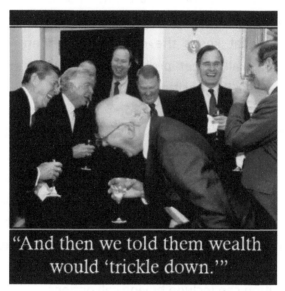

Picture: Bruce Howard.

"Bull markets" says Paul B Farrell at '*MarketWatch*,' "are based on Wall Street, connected through governments and are spread throughout global economic markets based on free market economic theory and the belief in perpetual growth. Perpetual growth through the old hierarchical belief system that is alive and well all over the world, "it's just the way things are" we are told. And many still listen..."

The problem with the present Bull Market, when looked at as a whole energy field system, is that much of the time it does not allow for 'sustainable regrowth'. That is, it does not activate or expand growth within the community allowing that community to continue to prosper independently or collectively through its own collaborative, sustainable and traditional exchange work for reward ethic; it does not re-invest in its targeted community where traditional collective and tribal incomes are decimated by the over-lording often foreign free trade investors, who not only take most of the profit for themselves, but also remove large amounts of capital from the country they have plundered. This, in effect, sucks the life-force out of any society it enters: it does not feed or add to the re-growth of that community.

Free trade and Bull markets generally decimate the delicate balance of community spirit in any place they enter, taking people like Gerardo Arias Camacho away from the only livelihood they know by destroying their mutually co-operative work and living environment. Wrecking his ability to support his family, taking away the fruits of his labour, his independence and his future potential.

The question is, do the wonder-minds of finance, Wall Street, the IMF, World Bank etc., really get what's wrong with the economy yet, or are these closed, hierarchical, competitive, and technologically focused systems working just fine because this is the way that suits them best?

Listening to the usual mindless rhetoric which issues from many financial advisors, corporate spokespersons, or highly paid consultants, obscures issues about who exactly is running this world: is it religious fanatics, the government, the world banking system or the International Monetary Fund? Lack of transparency in the working of government in many financial systems obscures processes that show clearly and unmistakably how the money is being shared, who is profiting and where the money is going.

Furthermore, how can the average person with mortgage repayments, rising interest rates, constantly rising food and utility prices possibly know what is really happening in the monetary systems? So many have been pushed down deep, submerged under decades of corporate greed, asset stripping, wage cuts and insidious manoeuvres by banks and finance companies. Really, we can be forgiven for thinking we have no personal power or ability to make changes to the increasing take-over and domination of free trade and Bull market enterprises.

CHAPTER NINE

Managing Finances to Your Advantage

"The illiterate of the 21st century will not be those who cannot read and write, but those who cannot learn, unlearn and relearn." Alvin Toffler

What is the fundamental error of the human financial reward for work system that creates such devastating loss to the majority of people, enveloping whole society's in tidal waves of misery? Do we need to look more closely at where the current economy is taking us, and, more to the point, at who continues to benefit from the massive despair it generates? And is the old hierarchical belief system the whole problem?

'"Listen closely" continues Farrell. "America's big problem is our "sequestered" brains. Meaning: "to remove, isolate, set apart, retire, and withdraw into solitude." Think post-trauma stress, paralysis, and amnesia, lobotomized, entranced or just plain irrational. You're out of it; you're incapable of acting rationally.

And it's not just you: Economists, politicians and media pundits all have sequestered brains. They blab on endlessly about this or that, of their special interests hiding among the trillion-dollar war-and-peace sequester cuts. Blab on and on. Myopic.

Why? Their brains are sequestered too. Millions of noisy brains. But you can't hear them, no matter what. Your brain which is on a different frequency, only hears your set channels. …..This is also why 152 nations worldwide as well as America can't see the light at the end of the tunnel. Why we're blindly driving headlong into a massive economic and market collapse. Why do we refuse to see it? Why? Our collective brain periodically goes through these cycles, in the economy, markets, drama and in our personal lives. But our sequestered brains can't hear, never learn…"

But all is not lost. It is highly likely that we do not see these things because we do not know where to look, but the structure of four energy fields, or the lack of their complete traits as shown in illustration 1, allows us to see which aspects are manipulating and controlling our finances and therefore our lives. On the other hand, if our financial dealings are being managed to our advantage, then the energy field structure as described in illustration 2 will clearly show it. Not only that, but through this structure we will be able to judge the real value of a business, or any other system for that matter, to see whether it is working for the advantage of the community or not. We can determine whether the business system you use is just another scheme to rob you of your hard earned cash or is it actually supporting you in your personal and social communications, while assisting your community to achieve financial success?

The energy field structure permits us to view any business operating system, then judge whether they perform in a transparent and interconnected way or they will reveal if, where, and how you are being negatively affected by multinationals or Bull markets. Despite the power of the system, we, as humankind have been locked into for eons, our sequestered brains can wake up and push old structures out of the way. New business ethics, such as those activated by RealStew, are helping people with little or no experience with money to become financially awakened: to work, to earn to become independent, and ultimately to be in control of their own lives.

Loans through this system will be available on a low 1 percent or no interest user-friendly basis, and support systems will be plentiful. This may sound unreal or too good to be true, but the old hierarchical financial systems based on limited human capacity have had their day, and the new is here to replace the old.

As thoughts of a changing economy ran through my mind, a memory tugged at me from a small incident that occurred many years earlier that demonstrates the power in each of us. The following experience impacted on me as to why the financial situation is worth thinking about, because how each of us reacts to find real solutions during difficult times matters greatly to the larger human system.

CHAPTER TEN

You don't need to be a Rocket Scientist

"The best way to escape from a problem is to solve it."
Alan Saporta

The power we have over our own lives, that power which lies within each of our actions, was reinforced to me one day when I tripped over a piece of broken concrete on the pavement. Normally I would have reacted automatically to save myself from pain, by putting my arms out as I fell but at that moment I decided to stay aware and to fully experience the fall.

Instead of allowing my mind to block the pain that I was trying to avoid, I decided to stay fully aware in that moment: on making that decision I immediately went into slow mode, as though I'd entered into a time tunnel. I began to see every action clearly and feel every feeling I was having, all the while examining everything in slow motion as it occurred: will I fall and hurt both hands and arms or will I just let myself fall on my right hand and save myself any pain to the left – no, that's not a good idea because I'm right handed, and need my right hand to do stuff and function properly ... on and on went the debate in my mind, time seeming to last forever.

What a viewer of this accident would see as a quick fall, became a long process of decision making for me ... I finally decided to use my left arm only to break my fall. And my left arm really did take some punishment that day!

So what, who cares, you might say. What's that got to do with the economy?

It made me understand that while this was a simple fall and a painful one at that, it also became a great opportunity; allowing me to question my reality of time and space and how I could impact on the physical world. It taught me that I didn't have to simply react mindlessly to my experiences and environment, and it demonstrated in a real way that no matter what I did it might hurt, but I could still affect the outcome of whatever I was experiencing.

I began to slow down and apply this reasoning to many problems in my life, including my finances. Instead of 'just reacting' to debt or hardship, I stopped listening to those who repeated well-worn beliefs and mantras of the social norms, and learnt to place value on the questions that were trying to push through to the surface of my own mind. I accepted the fact that with more intention and awareness, despite the fact that I appear to be as insignificant in the greater scheme of things as a butterfly in a forest, or a bee in Mr Ingram's hives, what I do with my tiny wings *can affect a greater reality*. Instead of questioning whether or not I could live a better more fulfilled life, I began looking at ways to *create* change in my own part of the woods. And subsequently, realized how if many more people did this, our combined efforts could affect real change to everything, not only the whole financial environment!

It then became abundantly clear to me that those in charge of global finance understand this too; they understand very clearly how you and I in difficulty and at odds within our own lives, are playing right into their hands. The fact that our brains have been sequestered works very well to keep us tied to old patterns of survival and panic. When the price of coffee and other policies were affecting the life of Gerardo Arias Camacho, and his family, and when there is an influx of youth into the prison system, the end result is a distorted culture created by the prevailing global financial policy. These policies affect us all in every way, and as we shall see coffee prices, prisons and credit cards are bad enough, but they are not the worst of it by far. Because Free Trade policy is creeping into every aspect of society to affect the food we eat, which health care we receive, and the education of our children.

This understanding prompted me to spend some time researching further allegations of corporate greed and control, leading me to seriously wonder whether those in charge of global financial systems really understood or cared about the worries and fears of the average person.

Apparently they don't – as their public persona indicates. They are happy to continue dominating and controlling monetary policy, and manipulating the will of the people.

Many large corporations don't acknowledge or care that having a 'healthy economy' means you must liken the economy to a healthy family. Rather than providing for an entity called 'the family', the interests of 'the individuals within the family' must be supported for the family to function as a healthy, happy and financially fulfilled unit, because 'the sum is only as great as its parts'. The needs of each person must be met in order for the family unit, or any system, to function effectively and productively. Similar to Gerardo and his family's coffee production and the way in which he was connected to his community through his work. Having the means to feed, house and educate his children gave Gerardo a workable, satisfying and purposeful lifestyle.

Understanding the human capacity for analytical and creative ability and with practical skills as proposed by Dr Robert Sternberg, and when aligned with the abundance of the planet, I had to wonder why so many basic financial problems and fluctuations of the economy were still affecting mostly those on the large lower end of the financial food chain. The fact is, that if business continues as usual then these desperate conditions will remain unsolved.

On the other hand, when we acknowledge, value and activate the wider range of human energy traits, those intangible characteristics such as mercy, empathy, inspiration and compassion we quickly raise our analytical, creative and practical intellectual capacity. In so doing, we raise the awareness of the planet to higher and greater levels of consciousness.

CHAPTER ELEVEN

The Potential for Greatness

"Grown-ups never understand anything for themselves, and it's tiresome for children to be always and forever explaining things to them." Antoine de Saint-Exupery

Einstein was considered a genius, because he was so far ahead in his understanding of many aspects of the mind and the brain, which many people attribute to his curiosity. He was able to put theory into practice by applying the intangible to the physical world. Moreover, because we, like Einstein, have brains that act like electrons, and, as shown in an energy field structure, if an electron absorbs enough energy, our minds will rise to higher levels of consciousness. And that no matter what else we do, that our intention matters.

If we intend to rise to a higher level of consciousness, then it would pay to be more curious: we will need to act with more interest and intent to comprehend what it is we don't yet understand.

A document published by the Investigation Clinica titled *'Evidence about the Power of Intention'* states " ...all living organisms emit a constant current of photons as a means to direct instantaneous nonlocal signals from one part of the body to another and to the outside world. Biophotons are stored in the intracellular DNA.

When the organism is sick changes in the biophotons emissions are produced. Direct intention manifests itself as an electric and magnetic energy producing an ordered flux of photons. Our intentions seem to operate as highly coherent frequencies capable of changing the molecular structure of matter. For the intention to be effective it is necessary to choose the appropriate time. In fact, living beings are mutually synchronized (to each other) and to the earth and its constant changes of magnetic energy.

It has been shown that the energy of thought can also alter the environment. Hypnosis, stigmata phenomenon and the placebo affect can also be considered as types of intention, as instructions to the brain during a particular state of consciousness. Cases of spontaneous cures or remote healing of extremely ill patients represents instances of an exceedingly great intention to control diseases menacing our lives. The intention to heal the body, as well as the beliefs of the sick person, question the efficacy of the influences which promote healing... In conclusion, studies on thought and consciousness are emerging as fundamental aspects and not as mere epiphenomena that are rapidly leading to a profound change in the paradigms of Biology and Medicine."

Taking into account the potential of a child, it matters that we understand this phenomena as it applies to ourselves, and how these energies remain available within us all. So we can begin to allow for, and express the fullness of our possibilities to follow our own business and lifestyle dreams, to do so within a business and banking system that supports our individual growth.

You don't need to be a rocket scientist to understand or comprehend that this earth, a place with every conceivable outcome or possibility for human genius, love, inspiration, benevolence and compassion, is now locked into a deficient structure of desperate financial upheaval brought about through endless cycles of cultural and gender greed and entitlement based on a collective agreement and over valuation of a limited number of human energy traits. It is only when we activate our whole brain, mind and energy connection that personal and global systems can be transformed from the predatory collusion and domination of a few, to the bountiful expression of the whole: the whole body, the whole mind, the whole use of energy fields that raises the consciousness of all life.

We are past the point of questioning our limitations; we are at the point where it is time to take action, to expand our minds to meet the intangible needs of our soul, to activate change and regain balance in our social, financial, personal and global environments: it is time to ask ourselves the question that the great controllers fear: "what can I do about it?"

CHAPTER TWELVE

Changing the Economy? Your Voice Makes a Difference

"Of course the game is rigged but don't let that stop you. If you don't play, you can't win."
Robert A. Heilien

Freedom of the public mind is the killer of control. Those who seek power and domination over other people first of all work through fear to control information so they can control the public mind. Hitler was able to induce fear to dominate an unfulfilled German population against Europe after the first world war when Nazi Germany felt justified in going to war against those who were thought to be persecuting them financially; Nazi Germany under Hitler's domination and against the will of many German people, believed also that they were genetically superior; that they were entitled and had a right to control all others.

I know this is old news, but controlling the populace is the name of the game. Similarly the USA was able to use fear tactics against the will of many of its citizens to create support to go to war against Saddam Hussein. Under the guise of searching for weapons of mass destruction, George Bush participated in a war in order to maintain the control of oil in Iraq

We may be tired of hearing about it, nevertheless the power of the media and of political ideology to manipulate whole populations cannot be under estimated. Governments can and do push their own sinister agendas and many journalists publish stories which are not backed up with real facts thus circulating ideological concepts that support their own political beliefs.

Those in power in the British, United States and German governments compelled their citizens into years of brutal conflict during World War Two. Also, the involvement of United States in the Iraq and Vietnam wars remain as timeless examples of how those who have power will use it to their advantage. Their actions demonstrate how the most powerful nations in the world use the most blatant, influential means through corrupt leadership, and how it can go so terribly wrong.

The following information is from www.leadingtowar.com 'Bush Administration Claims Vs. The Facts'

"The Bush administration made a series of claims (as recent governments are doing) prior to the Iraq War, each intended to support the idea that Saddam Husseln was a grave and imminent threat. None of these claims were true.

Here, each of these claims is examined in detail, using government and press reports, to show how the Bush administration presented intelligence to support these claims, despite the fact that behind closed doors Bush officials knew this intelligence to be disputed or even false.

Eight Pre-War Claims Refuted

• No weapons of mass destruction of any kind were found in Iraq.

• No mobile biological weapons labs were found in Iraq.

• Iraq did not seek to acquire yellowcake uranium from Africa.

• The aluminum tubes were not suitable for nuclear weapons development.

• Mohamed Atta, the lead 9/11 hijacker, did not meet with Iraqi intelligence in Prague.

• Iraq did not provide chemical weapons training to al-Qaeda.

• There was no collaborative relationship between Iraq and al-Qaeda.

• The implication that Iraq was involved in the attacks of 9/11 was untrue.

The Costs of War:

Further, the Bush administration's assurances of how the war would unfold prove to be completely inaccurate where the ramifications of the Iraq War have been tragic:

- After four years, the American invasion and occupation of Iraq has brought with it more than 100,000 civilian and military deaths.
- Millions of Iraqis have been displaced from their homes. Nearly 2,000,000 have fled the country.
- Untold numbers of people have been mentally and physically wounded.
- War expenditures have (far) exceeded $500 billion."

Misguided or not, inciting fear, lack of finance and lack of freedom are excuses for war. War traditionally means the reaping of huge benefits for many large companies. In the past, the more pressure people were put under, the more they would react to powerful and inciting rhetoric from master manipulators.

By mindlessly reacting, communities fall further and deeper into the old pattern of conflict and chaos. This model of leadership continues today as the fear of terrorism is expanded and used by governments and companies to gain greater power through the control of weapons, which in turn incites fear of infiltration. It is here that we must ask ourselves "Has the build-up of global military power been activated for public safety, or for the benefit of financial institutions and Bull Markets?"

CHAPTER THIRTEEN

Conspiracies?

"After everything I've been through, the last thing I'm going to apologize for is my paranoia."
Richard Finney

The term, *'conspiracy,'* is bandied about in conjunction with words such as 'secret plot, racket, scheme, cabal, insider trading, or dealing,' but what does this mean for us in terms of actual application and the effect that recent financial policy has on people's lives and families now? You would wonder why we need to even consider the cost of financial conspiracies in terms of human misery, not only to avoid repeating the folly of World War Two or the Iraq war scenario, but to effect *real* change for ourselves, our environment, and the future of human wellbeing these things must be considered if real change is to happen.

Michael Kelly, a Washington Post journalist and critic of anti-war movements on both the left and right, coined the term "fusion paranoia" to refer to a political convergence of left-wing and right-wing activists around anti-war issues and civil liberties, which he said were motivated by a shared belief in conspiracism or anti-government views.

Or is it more as Daniel Pipes wrote in a *Jerusalem Post* article titled *Fusion Paranoia:* "Fears of a petty conspiracy – a political rival or business competitor plotting to do you harm – are as old as the human psyche. But fears of a grand conspiracy – that the Illuminati or Jews plan to take over the world – go back only 900 years and have been operational for just two centuries, since the French Revolution. "Conspiracy Theories" grew in importance from then until World War II, when two arch-conspiracy theorists, Hitler and Stalin, faced off against each other, causing the greatest blood-letting in human history... '…. Some historians have put forward the idea that more recently the United States has become the home of conspiracy theories because so many high-level prominent conspiracies have been undertaken and uncovered since the 1960s." The existence of such real conspiracies helps feed the belief in "conspiracy theories."

Katherine K. Young states "the fact remains, however, that not all conspiracies are imagined by paranoids. Historians show that every real conspiracy has had at least four characteristic features:

- Groups not isolated individuals

- Illegal or sinister aims, not ones that would benefit society as a whole
- Orchestrated acts, not a series of spontaneous and haphazard ones
- Secret planning, not public discussion." *Wikipedia*

When there is a gap in the universe then something will fill it. And unless a better system is created to replace old egocentric forces, then the same corrupt structures will simply replace them – but they will show up in a different form. And unless we replace the existing ineffectual business models with new models incorporating fundamental changes, then nothing will improve, and we will keep on getting what we have always got.

The World Bank lends money to counteract poverty through the work of aid agencies all over the world. They support devastated and poor areas, but also countries with phenomenal natural wealth, which have little or no underlying support structure for workers at the lower end of the financial spectrum. Yet again, the wealth extracted from these countries is not distributed fairly to locals working in the industries.

For example Africa's vast natural resources, of minerals and diamond mines that are owned and operated by big corporations remove billions of dollars from the economy. In many cases, not even a fraction of its income is distributed to the local community, let alone the whole country. These corporations have been decimating Africa and its assets, through their ongoing corrupt practices which are aided and abetted through local business interests and are often in collusion with the International Monetary Fund and the World Bank.

All this gives rise to a more troubling question which is, does the mere fact that we as observers are living and complying within the present system, are we energizing these dinosaur incompetent and corrupt methods? Are we by default colluding in the strength and growth of global poverty entrapment through silent participation?

Most important as Christopher Houghton Budd from the Centre of Associative Economics asks "Do we need to understand right now, whether economics as we understand it is fit for modern economic life?"

Is it time to change old brain methods and old world thinking? Those promoting actions that not only affect us financially but are working to enforce the closure of local information and resources, therefore interfering with free communication of whole populations globally? But, more to the point how can we as free individuals continue with a dinosaur mentality where, apart from asking the question why do we continue on in these systems? We need to find out where and how to bring about change, and to quote Einstein, to consider how "The answers are now different".

CHAPTER FOURTEEN

Energy Fields and Financial Theories

"The use of solar energy has not been opened up because the oil industry does not own the sun." Ralph Nader

Individual economists and visionaries have been asking similar questions and applying a different reasoning. However because I knew little about financial reasoning or conspiracies at that time, it was easier for me to put *all* financial theories into the system I did understand which involved a great deal about human thinking patterns, and how to merge and expand them into greater and healthier levels of consciousness; consequently, the energy field system has been constantly refined and expanded as I work with it to find the answers I need.

Through the basic interactive characteristics it takes to run healthy physical, emotional, mental and spiritual networks, we need all energy traits to interact and to function well, which enables us to live our lives with clearer and happier relationships, and with a more profound sense of being. Then we can, with greater intention activate these fields *consciously* through personal energy field awareness.

While discovery of this system was in the interests of healing on an individual level, as explained in my book *The Structure of Energy Healing*, I found these traits to be necessary and vital aspects to build healthier more interactive and caring cultures, where they are vital to establishing more humane societies *and* financial institutions. It is not difficult to see that all traits in the structure of consciousness are equally valuable to the foundation of the interactive and variable nature of humanity.

Not only are all traits inherent within all of us, but there are higher and lower, or denser and finer levels of left and right brain activity. These different energy patterns show a new model of human intelligence which is only now being understood when explaining the human mind, intelligence and social factors.

Many energy field functions which maintain a healthy structure have long been seen by the old thought system as impossible, vague or weak, and of no importance or value to business or society. A strict and unyielding belief system has grown around this conviction in which all energy - physical, emotional, mental and spiritual is held tightly and controlled by a few within the present power elite of businessmen, scientists and social commentators.

However, this is a grave misunderstanding and abuse of life-force and human intelligence, and what is becoming unmistakably clear is how this limited thinking has allowed some traits to become more powerful in the structure of the global economy and how it has demeaned others. Those neglected energies, which we are aware are becoming more and more necessary in global business and political life.

Innocence	Compassion
Curiosity	Protector
Inspiration	Divine Love
Mercy	Empathy
Active	Nurturing
Masculine	Feminine
Logical	Intuitive
Competitive	Passive
Independent	Interdependent
Closed	Transparent
Hierarchical	Inclusive

Illustration 3

It is easy to see that the dominating power structure of *physical activity, independent, competitive, hierarchical and closed* systems have been singled out as the most valuable. Humanity therefore has been elevating these particular traits above all others. Because of this, they have become the prevailing energies to aspire to. In energy field terms, this means that by holding, or submitting, to those values, individuals, societies and global business concerns are being confined to the rules and controls of that one field.

The energy field structure shows clearly how the present dysfunctional financial systems carry a very limited range of human intelligence. The few aspects that are in charge at this time are only a small part in a wide ranging and endless field of human capabilities, but they have grown through organisation and violence over the last eight to ten thousand years into the ruling force.

As a result most communities are sadly lacking in the care and welfare of their inhabitants creating severe imbalances in many societies. Inequalities which could have been avoided have resulted through poor distribution of resources and wealth, along with an immense loss of basic human rights for individuals.

No matter what the financial system is or its content, the energy field structure pinpoints very quickly and clearly where any system fails to meet the needs of its people, where it is lacking in their actual 'human traits', or more to the point what is missing in their *structure of consciousness*. At a glance it can be seen how these traits affect our life and environment and distinctions can be made when certain aspects are missing, as to which systems are supportive and constructive and lead to higher consciousness, as opposed to those which on their own become destructive and negative often lacking any consciousness at all.

When considering humankind's brain/mind connection, potential and possible intellectual activity we are beginning to understand that one section of our awareness cannot do it all. Sadly, we are able to see right now where millions of people whose dreams of a great financial future are being shattered, because they are locked into the present limited and unhealthy hierarchical power systems, that have resulted only in the growth of scarcity, chaos and fear, all of which ultimately lead to conflict.

CHAPTER FIFTEEN

Youth Unemployment

Student: *"Dr. Einstein, aren't these the same questions in last year's (physics) final?"*
Einstein: *"Yes, but this year the answers are different."*

Adherence to old financial belief systems keeps many people cut off from their traditional social connections and environment because of the lack of meaningful work available to them. More and more young people are disconnecting from their community, too many lacking in fulfilment of their dreams and purpose, ultimately finding no reason to even get up in the morning. Some like 18 year old Joel O'Loughlan who says in the following report, "I've handed out over 50 CVs since January. Each day I go to the job centre and look online as well. I've had two interviews but I didn't get either job. You don't even get a call back most of the time. It makes you feel ... I don't know, like, what's the point?"

Joel is only one of millions of young men and women who are becoming more and more despondent as their lack of employment and income prevents them from functioning in what should be a vital connection to their natural social base. Then in their frustration, they begin making less desirable connections to regain the self-acknowledgement and identity they were born with; supplementing their despair by taking drugs, acting out sexually or through antisocial and self-destructive acts: many drifting through life without real purpose, ensnared within diverse political and religious factions that are fighting for control of resources to bolster warped political and religious ideologies.

Control over angry, dissatisfied individuals has led to the greatest escalations of violence in human history. For example, when you examine the stereotypes behind the conflict, the beliefs and the theories that accompany them, most conflicts are based on generally accepted dogma that favour and benefit very few; they benefit the agenda of those people who are in control at the top of the financial, religious or political game. Traditional business, political or religious fundamentalism is benefiting very few and you are twice as likely to be on the losing end of this game if you are young, female or black.

James Ball, Dan Milmo and Ben Ferguson in their report for 'The Guardian,' 9 March 2012, "Office for National Statistics (ONS) data show that half of UK's young black males are now unemployed.

Unemployment rate for black 16 to 24-year-olds available for work is now double that for white counterparts

The ONS (UK) says unemployment for young black male job seekers has risen from 28.8% in 2008 to 55.9% in the last three months of 2011, twice the rate for young white people. More than half of young black men available for work in Britain are now unemployed, according to unpublished government statistics obtained by the Guardian which show the recession is hitting young black people disproportionately hard: the youth unemployment rate for black people has increased at almost twice the rate for white 16 to 24year olds since the start of the recession in 2008. Young black men are the worst affected of all, according to a gender breakdown contained within the data supplied by the ONS".

What happens meanwhile with the increasing surplus of youth: 55% unemployed in Spain, where the general population who are unemployed is 20%? Or the 40% of extra Chinese and Indian males who are, or soon will be, coming into their high testosterone prime male power after decades of parental preferences for boys.

With an excess of young men, it means that they will be regularly forced or coerced into uninspiring work or military service. Or, sadly, will these young men understanding their own victimhood in the world of religious, political and financial inequality be left to their own devices and sexual appetites, free to roam the streets of the world? And who benefits?

As free trade progresses, private prison giant 'Corrections Corporation of America' gains ever greater power along with monolith Monsanto and its non-renewable seed monopoly. Similar to Monsanto, that by manipulating seed stocks, have destroyed the traditional ability of farmers to be self-sufficient. Where farmers used to use seed from their own crops to replant the following season, Monsanto's genetic engineering policy forces them to buy new seeds each season, which farmer's often cannot afford.

Like seeds denied growth, young people are jailed for minor drug offenses to feed Corrections of America's insatiable Bull Market. Where, in a recent tidal wave of new free trade based privately owned prison systems, younger, and younger people (mainly young men) are introduced quickly and brutally into a higher degree of criminal behaviour and more sinister levels of violence based crimes. What happens to the lives of these young men and women after a shocking and brutal introduction to the prison system?

CHAPTER SIXTEEN

A Bull Position?

"Overcoming poverty is not a task of charity, it is an act of justice."
Nelson Mandela

When a small a faction of energy traits gain too much power over the gentler and more vulnerable areas, this stifles human consciousness. As we have seen, when there is a break-down in social interaction, Bull Markets grow stronger. This means, in effect that the majority of people are losing power in their own lives, their choices are diminishing, leaving many unable to express and manifest the inspirational thoughts of their own consciousness. This is a bit like being caught in one part of the system that has a cancer which dominates then spreads to infect the wellbeing of the whole person. Such an early dysfunction affects a person for the rest of their life.

Why on earth do people keep feeding Bull markets which are based on scarcity for the majority and abundance for a few? Paul Farrell continues "It's why we're blindly driving headlong into a massive economic and market collapse. Why do we refuse to see it? Why?

Our collective brain periodically goes through these cycles, in the economy, markets, drama, in our personal lives. But our sequestered brains can't hear, so they never learn..."

Moreover, human energy field systems that were once healthy and connected workable structures are now driving blindly down a road which while being extremely uncomfortable has become shockingly familiar; feeding into the mouths of dominant Bull Markets: markets that have become self-replicating cultural, business and financial dictatorships infecting generations. Like old Chinese warlords who have controlled the ability of many generations to achieve self-sufficiency, by repeatedly enforcing closed systems of violence and control on the population down through the ages.

The present global market place is no different; all it has done has changed form as it went on from local politics to gain momentum in a global market.

Is this anything like the business or government policy you've been hearing lately? Governmental warlords pushing closed business agendas of free trade agreements into the public domain. James Ball, Dan Milmo and Ben Ferguson continue. "Iqbal Wahhab, owner of the Roast restaurant in London and chair of the ethnic minority advisory group at the Department for Work and Pensions, said the (unemployment) figures had exposed an issue that has been "like the elephant in the room". Wahhab, who runs his own mentoring scheme for young black youths, urged the government to join businesses in tackling the problem. "Now that the figures are out in the public domain, what are we going to do about it?"

He added: "I would love to see ministers doing more. If it is businesses doing it, that's great, because we are more in tune with how to make programs run efficiently, but we need to see how the government is going to reverse that tide."

The reaction among black youths on the streets of Toxteth, the Liverpool district that saw some of the worst inner-city riots of the Thatcher era was one of frustration like Joel who added: "Being black definitely makes it harder. Sometimes if you're going to a job [the employers] look at you like you're not going to work here, they think you're not the right kind of person. That's across the board. I've been handing CVs out to coffee shops, shops, you name it. I need the money and will go to uni to do what I really want next year but right now it feels like more than bad luck..."

Where do these young people go now? What are their options when one energy field is still controlling the life flow of their potential? They exist in a distorted energy field structure which continues to uphold the supremacy of the most powerful through the control of money flow and through cultural and religious persecution. A severe political policy maintains authority, suppressing any minority groups striving to make their voices heard.

One aspect of our mind absorbs the effect this is having on the economy, the economy which affects not only the spending ability of the average Joe or Jane worker, but the entire wellbeing of their family as well. As no part of our lives are unaffected, there is the fear that in the wider scheme of things with the current global plague of dominant markets and few alternatives, numerous people will become unemployed. Sadly, this leaves many feeling powerless and frustrated because of their inability to make free and authentic choices. Many lose homes, some starve, peace talks fail, and law and justice in the community breaks down – all in the name of free trade.

To top it all off, governmental mouths drag out old beliefs still held by many, in which family and cultural successes or failures are a series of events imprinted directly from the gods, or, depending on the culture you live in, like the caste system in India a fixed part of your DNA. Lack of social order tends to stem largely from reinforced prejudices of global extremes within the old, tired and lopsided unworkable Energy Field Structures.

When the physically stronger traits dominate all areas of the financial spectrum, then the emotional, mental and spiritual aspects of life are also profoundly out of balance. This works in reverse also. Dominating traits have fed for generations on the energy of the physically weaker more vulnerable aspects of their particular social environments.

Try it now, put the system that is troubling you most up against the energy field structure and see which traits are most dominant, and which are absent.

Moreover, it shows how the need for charity, prison systems and aid to the poor is the creation of a distorted spread of wealth and misguided ideology. Charity or bigger prison systems are not the answer nor are they viable as a long term solution to these ongoing problems, especially when much of the currency donated to charities is siphoned off by intermediaries or those at the top end of the receiving line who can control its flow. Not only is crime or charity, except in cases of extreme hardship, natural disaster or destruction, simply another manifestation of the old unworkable system of hierarchy and scarcity within human consciousness, but it creates ongoing social problems through financial dependency and social separation.

These traits are clearly running throughout whole environments and the global energy financial system, where instead of educating or financing people into work or into empowerment and self-sufficiency, upside-down financial markets are turning people into lower class citizens. They become charity cases, heretics or criminals, thus enabling the present growth in inequality and criminal activity which results in additional convictions, further enforcing a strong warlord prison culture. This in turn further *promotes* the strength and growth of Bull Market investments. Through government officials and Washington lobbyists, these miserable developments become self-benefitting laws.

CHAPTER SEVENTEEN

Prisons and Bull Markets: You do the Math

"I don't want yes-men around me. I want everybody to tell me the truth even if it costs them their jobs." Samuel Goldwyn

Fareed Zakaria in *Time* magazine April 2 2011 cites the growing concern of the latest US criminal statistics when in 1980 the United States' prison population was about 150 per 100,000 it has quadrupled since then. So something has happened to push millions of Americans into prisons.

That something of course was the war on drugs. Drug convictions since 1980 went from 15 inmates per 100,000, to 146 in 1998, an almost tenfold increase... In 2009 1.66 million Americans were arrested on drugs charges. And *4 out of 5* of those charges were simply for possession.

Then there is the political and Bull Market money trail, where many state prisons are run by private companies with powerful lobbyists in state capitols. The state of California in 2011 spent $US9.6 billion on prisons vs. $5.7 billion on state colleges. Since 1980, California has built one college campus and twenty one prisons. A college student costs the state $8,667 per year; a prisoner costs $45,000 a year. The results are gruesome at every level. Americans are creating a vast prisoner underclass in the country at huge expense. Inmates and ex-prisoners become increasingly unable to function in normal society. Americans are creating a vast prisoner underclass in the country at huge expense, with people increasingly unable to function in normal society, all in the name of a war they've already lost.

Prisons?

You do the math.

In a capitalist, free trade market USA laws are being exported to places like New Zealand, Australia and Europe and most of the world, which further the imbalance of wealth and all areas of health and law. Many of these laws create only piece meal solutions which are no solution at all. Large social problems are inappropriately dumped into the individual's own personal space. So now, hardworking people like unemployed Joel and small businessman Gerardo are subject to the system's demands which have created such an upheaval within their culture that mental and emotional problems now explode within whole populations. And ask yourself, who benefits from that, apart from prisons and large multinational drug companies?

Real solutions are being ignored as tons of medication is dispensed to younger and younger people. Large prison sentences are imposed for minor crimes, and mental health problems have become endemic globally. As a result, the current profit flowing to the providers of medication, their investors, the company directors and the shareholders built into Bull Markets is huge, and they are laughing all the way to the bank.

How is it that the imbalance of power, that feeds wealth into the hands of an already wealthy elite minority, continues to dominate the daily lives of those less fortunate? Where individuals and groups on the lower rungs of the social and financial ladder are subject to these shameful dominating business influences: where our sequestered brains are allowed to blab on endlessly through set channels in our psyche, in our mind-set, even in our soul as it is sequestered too, and we all lapse into a trance, confused.

Perpetual growth has become the mantra as individual societies are controlled more and more by outside forces while increased free trade pressures, designed to feed the myth of perpetual growth at all cost, flourish. The lack of humanity this agenda promotes further degrades the breakdown of societies and local communities, but ultimately, the lives and spirit of its people.

The big question is, "why has this paradigm been able to continue for so long at the expense of humanity's wellbeing?"

CHAPTER EIGHTEEN

Humanity's Wellbeing: Maintaining Growth in Dysfunctional Systems

"I guess I should warn you, if I turn out to be particularly clear, you've probably misunderstood what I've said."
Alan Greenspan

Many systems such as Communism or Socialism have tried and eventually failed to build and promote healthy global structures. None were able to maintain growth, because their own limited agendas generally got in the way of people's freedom and inspiration; the agenda that drives those at the top of most political systems to stay in control, eventually stifles the growth of inspiration in less powerful individuals.

Through social control or lack of stimulating leadership these systems fail to support people to achieve their greatest potential. They fail to provide sustainable economic growth. A free trade Capitalist system works on the tenet of the freedom of people to grow and aspire to great wealth which is based on the premise of perpetual growth at all cost. But is growth for its own sake, at the cost of people's welfare and great environmental damage, the answer?

Paul B. Farrell says, "Driving the 'economists' growth myth is population growth. It's the independent variable in their equation. Population growth is what drives all other derivative projections, forecasts and predictions. All GDP growth, income growth, wealth growth, production growth, everything. These unscientific growth assumptions fit into the overall left-brain, logical, mind-set of western leaders, all the corporate CEOs, Wall Street bankers and government leaders who run America and the world.

But just because a large group collectively believes in something doesn't make it true. Perpetual growth is still a myth no matter how many economists, CEOs, bankers and politicians believe it. It's still an illusion trapped in the brains of all these irrational, biased and uncritical people... Grow OR Die. Traditional economists (pro-capitalism): We're told we need 3% GDP growth to support the next batch of 100 million Americans. We believe it on faith. Drill Baby Drill. Buy stuff. Get new jobs to fuel growth. We're out of control. Exploding growth fuels demands as the rest of the world adds 2.9 billion new humans, all chasing their "American dream."

When looked at as a whole, it is clear that excessive growth of just one of the four energy fields demonstrates that reliance on perpetual expansion in one area (any area) causes the depletion of growth in the other three fields. An imbalance is created by the bulge, disrupting the health and wellbeing of the whole system: the energy field system, whether it is representing an individual person or a business structure, is a vital component in the matrix which together make up a complete and complex social order, capable of generating its own life-force. The life force, which in turn feeds nourishment back into itself. Real and fundamental change occurs if and when economists are willing to concede that all traits must co-operate in order for an individual organism to thrive.

"Grow AND Die," continues Farrell. "This mean that New eco-economists (environmentalists) see Big Oil's destruction of our coastal economies, the rape of West Virginia's coal mountains, the unintended consequences of uncontrolled carbon emissions and they ask: "When will economists, politicians and corporate leaders stop pretending Earth's resources are infinitely renewable?

Yes, our world is at a crossroads, facing a dilemma, confronting the ultimate no-win scenario, because the "Myth of Perpetual Growth" is essential to support the global population explosion. But all this "Growth" is also killing our world, wasting our planet's non-renewable natural resources. "Eternal Growth" is suicidal and will eventually destroy the Earth. We're damned if we grow. Damned if we don't".

In terms of energy fields, eternal growth means continually feeding the lower left energy field – needing more and more fodder for the hungry, greedy Bull that is sucking more life-force and energy from the wider community. More and more young people will be thrown into prisons systems or led into needless battle. More and more people like Gerardo and Terence will be sacrificed to the system.

"Future economists will be forced into 'No-Growth' Economics. But will economists change as long as they're mercenaries in the employ of Perpetual Growth Capitalists? No. It will take a new mind-set. The difference between the mind-set of traditional economists and the new eco-economists is simple: Traditional economists think short-term, react short-term, and pursue short-term goals. New eco-economists think long-term. Initially this may seem overly simplistic, but fits perfectly. Here's why: Old traditional economists — short-term thinkers: Traditional economists are employees and consultants for organizations with short-term views — banks, big corporations, institutional investors, think-tanks, government. They all think in lock-step, driven by daily returns, quarterly earnings, and annual bonuses. Short business and election cycles are more important than what happens a decade in the future. Their brains are convinced: If we can't survive the short-term, long-term is irrelevant.

Environmental economists — long-term thinkers: New eco-economists see, think and plan for the long-term. They know that the traditional economists' and capitalists' way of thinking and advising is setting America up for more and bigger catastrophes than the Gulf oil spill and the last meltdown. The "Avatar" film is a perfect metaphor: Soon capitalism will exhaust Earth's resources forcing us to invade distant planets searching for new energy resources".

When life-force is withdrawn from the energy fields of a healthy human body, those fields, like flowers in the desert lose consciousness wither and die. We see this around the world when people who lack the means to be self-sufficient as when private companies such as Wal-Mart enter their community. When they are unable to align to their working environment, those communities then wither and die in the same way. A great example of this occurs in the food chain when the western diet of corporate processed foods is introduced into traditional indigenous populations, disease and illnesses which had been unknown in the past, spread quickly throughout the community.

In the seventies, Physician T.L. Cleave, a surgeon captain with the Royal Navy and director of research of

Navel Medicine discovered this fact and published an epidemiological study called *The Saccharine Disease*. He noted how Yemenite Jews after arriving from Yemen and living twenty years on a western diet in Israel gained diseases such as obesity, diabetes and colon cancer which became all too apparent in the community. After forty years these diseases were widespread through the population. Cleave came to call it 'the rule of twenty years', whereby he found in his travels that any population after being introduced to a western diet would become progressively ill. Sick individuals then create a sick society.

Similarly, that sick societies create sick individuals. Why would we want to inflict unworkable financial policies on anyone: why send an unworkable financial system onto other galaxies when it is clearly failing in its own orbit? Especially when it is known that combined energy field traits are paramount to all interactive human activities. The individual parts of any system whether it is diet or finances must be physically, emotionally, mentally and spiritually healthy and satisfied in its own orbit, in order to connect wholly and work consciously not only for its own benefit, but for the benefit of the whole society.

It makes sense that if individuals are unable to be self-sustaining in their own orbit, they will be unable to meet their own needs let alone the requirements of their family and community. Disempowering the individual renders the whole system faulty. Like a malignant cell in the human body, lack of concern for each person affects all parts of the energy chain and to varying degrees the community functions less effectively. It is then that corruption like any other miserable virus is able to take over and greater degrees of difficulty are likely to follow. Like a global malignant cancer cell, the likelihood of conflict increases as exploitation grows, leading humanity into deeper levels of disease, poverty and war.

Balance is not only profoundly necessary for the growth and health of all life, but the denial of life-force to those who are working at the grass roots level will eventually cause the whole unit to collapse. Like the colony collapse disorder (CCD) of Mr. Ingram's hives, or the foundation of any house, the base must be strong enough to sustain its own weight. As we see now, the majority of the world's inhabitants are weakening financially, while they support the wealth and habits of a top heavy one percent.

CHAPTER NINETEEN

Investing in Transparency and Accountability

"There are many highly successful businesses in the United States. There are also many highly paid executives. The policy is not to confuse the two." Norman R. Augustine

The US financial system, like the rest of the globe, has become as unhealthy in its lending and borrowing to poorer nations as it is to its own population, where US debt is increasing faster than the medical bills in the community. Prescription drug spending rose to $307.4 billion in 2010, which translates into nearly $900 for every American, as reported by the IMS? Health in the United States Review of 2010.

What is clear, is that an independent and collective financial system is vital to activate human awareness, to break away from the present dynamics of a global financial structure which perpetrates mistreatment for many. Such patronizing and persecuting of the most vulnerable overpowers natural curiosity and annihilates individual inspiration, producing systems that never worked well or effectively for anybody in the first place. These are the consequences of systems like communism, socialism and free-trade ventures, which expanded into larger structures of global corruption through exorbitant, self-interested lending, borrowing and controlling tactics.

Joseph Hanlon and Ann Pettifor in *Kicking the Habit,* highlight a way to tackle corruption by providing more just, democratic and transparent procedures by calling for more independent, accountable and transparent methods for managing relationships between sovereign debtors and their public and private creditors.

An independent process would have five goals:

• Restore some justice to a system in which international creditors play the role of plaintiff, judge and jury, in their own court of international finance.

• Introduce discipline into sovereign lending and borrowing arrangements—and thereby prevent future crises.

• Counter corruption in borrowing and lending, by introducing accountability through a free press and greater transparency to civil society in both the creditor and debtor nations.

• Strengthen local democratic institutions, by empowering them to challenge and influence elites.

• Encourage greater understanding and economic literacy among citizens, and thereby empower them to question, challenge and hold their elites to account."

These points show why systems which invest in transparency and accountability in small matters are more likely to support and empower those who are vulnerable in society; like protecting a butterfly in the forest, or a Bee in Mr Ingram's hives. As they invest in justice for each person, they are automatically strengthening justice in the community.

CHAPTER TWENTY

The Power of One

*"When I give food to the poor, they call me a saint.
When I ask why the poor have no food, they call me a
communist."*
Dom Hélder Câmara

"In Patna," writes Jyoti Thottam for *Time* magazine
November 7, 2011, "in the noisy capitol of India's
northern Bihar state, a crowd gathers early for the
weekly *janata darbar*, the "people's audience." Many
have travelled for hours, even days most are poor, a few
barefoot, each one has showed up for the same thing,
to present their grievances directly to Bihar's chief
minister, Nitish Kumar.

As each man is heard his request is dispatched by
clerk to the relevant officials, a group of ministers and
bureaucrats. The minister promises to look into it, and
the person is then able to track the progress of their
complaint online in their nearest town ... Petitioner Ram
Pandey a seventy five year old farmer is tracking his
right to water that has been diverted by an upstream
neighbor of a different caste ... Why did he make the

124-km journey to Janata Darbar? "If not here, then where?" he says. "We now have hope."

Nitish Kumar ran for the chief minister's job in 2005 promising only that "the rule of law will be established." While Kumar's rival promised jobs, state subsidies, empowerment of the lower castes, lawlessness had become so extreme that it trumped everything else.

Before, says police officer Ram Uday Tiwari. "You couldn't do anything. Everybody had some political connection. We were constantly getting orders not to file charge sheets against this person or that person." Now Tiwari spends his time doing his job investigating crimes, finding witnesses and holding public grievances meetings twice a week.

Kumar got the legislature to pass the Bihar Special Courts Act of 2009 which gives the right to confiscate the property of those charged with having "disproportionate assets" in excess of their income. Earlier this year law was applied for the first time when the house of an influential bureaucrat in Patna was seized. He denies the charge, and if he is acquitted he is entitled to the value of the property plus interest. If not the pale yellow house with the gaudy black metal gate will remain Pratmik Vidyalaya primary school.

There is also a time limit of one year for corruption trials so cases won't drag on as they are wont to do in

India. "It gives the feeling of instituting vigorous justice." says C.V.Madhukar of PRS Legislative Research, a governance institute based in New Delhi. "It's a very important signal."... As security has improved farmers are getting their grains and produce to market without fear of being robbed, shop keepers are staying open longer and people do not fear going out after dark. While economic gains are modest, deprivation has led to innovation. One program, replicated in several other states provides bikes to girls who enroll in ninth grade, an incentive that not only helps close the education gap but makes it less likely those girls will marry before age eighteen. Bihar is also the first state to fully implement a Right to Public Services Act, which puts a time limit on common public service requests, for example, 30 days for a driver's license. 60 days for a ration card. The law makes it more difficult for bureaucrats to wheedle bribes by delaying requests: a clerk who fails to provide a service in time has to personally pay the fee.

Bihar state has come this far largely because of Kumar. Will the changes endure after he departs the scene? Kumar says that the people will not allow Bihar to backslide. "There are two streams," he says. "One is that of cynicism, nothing can happen, while all the corruption is there. The parallel stream indicates that people have started having faith in better governance.

This kind of stream is also flowing. It will get wider and wider and ultimately the other one will diminish. One day nobody is going to tolerate corruption."

Energy field traits, give an immediate snap shot of what is happening in a community; what is affecting the wellbeing of the body, mind and spirit of an individual, a nation or indeed the planet. No matter what political, financial or religious beliefs are held Kumar brought about change in the Patna structure by activating justice through law and order amongst the people. Consequently, the workings of Patna became less corrupt and more nurturing toward all its inhabitants; how did he do this?

Kumar not only instigated aspects from both of the *lower* energy field spectrums into the structure of Patna's working life, but with traits such as *transparency, inclusiveness, and interdependence*, he activated the positive aspects of competition, hierarchy and logic. This set up a system of fair-mindedness to not only gain a foothold and gather life-force in the community, but for its people to flourish.

Innocence	Compassion
Curiosity	Protector
Inspiration	Divine Love
Mercy	Empathy
Active	Nurturing
Masculine	Feminine
Logical	Intuitive
Competitive	Passive
Independent	**Interdependent**
Closed	**Transparent**
Hierarchical	**Inclusive**

Illustration 4

You would have noticed (you did, didn't you?), that there was little mention of women in that report apart from the following sentence: "One program, replicated in several other states, provides bikes to girls who enrol in ninth grade, an incentive that not only helps close the education gender gap but makes it less likely those girls will marry before age eighteen".

No matter how much money is thrown at a social problem, nothing would improve a situation such as that which occurred in Patna if change in the energy field structure had not taken place. Imagine too, if Kumar had instigated all of the traits from the lower right quadrant into those reforms by giving value to the *female, passive* and *nurturing* traits along with those he did implement, the *interdependent, inclusive* and *transparent* qualities.

CHAPTER TWENTY-ONE

Valuing Precious Human Resources

"Energy is liberated matter, matter is energy waiting to happen."
Bill Bryson

Many traditional Indigenous cultures such as Maya, Australian Aboriginal, Native American and New Zealand Maori valued passive traits along with active qualities and by acknowledging those qualities Kumar would have awakened even higher aspects of consciousness into the community.

This would benefit Patna's dominant left brain social awareness, where caregivers in the village would be valued for their *compassionate, empathetic* qualities and many of the other gentle *passive and nurturing* skills. In most indigenous cultures women had great standing in the eyes of the community for their wisdom, their insights and their listening skills; skills that were esteemed and acknowledged for their positive impact on the community.

These traits are not defined solely by women. Traditional communities valued and maintained these more gentle and indefinable qualities for a wider purpose. They were the vehicle through which they retained and kept alive highly valued ancient information: it was acknowledged and understood that these more subtle areas held vital links to the ancestors and higher consciousness.

This illustrates the way in which a more transcendent consciousness has been lost to western society, which now perceives these feminine traits as merely for the weak, affording them very low status and little financial value. It has become an overpowering belief that prevents women and most ethnic groups from both receiving wealth and accumulating wealth. A lack of acknowledgement and value toward these more gentle and creative skills have also prevented many people from finding the self-fulfilment they search for, but never find, because feminine traits do not fit with their left brain oriented cultures.

Sadly, we see little evidence of these more humanising qualities entering business, because so many are caught up in competitive strategies for earning a living which enable them to 'keep up with the Joneses', as they step up the corporate ladder. Little reward or consideration is shown for the caregivers of the world; for their kindness, for their compassion and for their indispensable knowledge and skill. These are gifts to humanity which have become all but invisible, remaining largely unseen and sadly, unrecognized for their true worth.

"On the one hand", says Eric Toussaint in *Your Money or your Life*, "the capitalist system takes full advantage of a pre-existing form of oppression: patriarchy. At the same time, it accentuates the features of this oppression. Indeed, women's oppression is a weapon that capitalists use to control the workforce as a whole and even to justify their policies by shifting responsibility for social welfare from the state and collective institutions to the 'privacy' of the family".

Patriarchy is a system which flourishes today and which without our intervention will continue on into the future with little time or tolerance for equality, or interference to its power base. This leaves little room for whole-scale empathy and compassion to expand, and without these precious human resources humanity will stay locked into a deficient structure of consciousness. That is, we will continue to measure everything that is valuable in society solely in tunnel vision terms financially. Additionally, and most worrying of all, is how a lack of higher human energy field traits affects the most vulnerable in society.

It is vitally important to understand how patriarchy blocks the flow of human life-force toward families and how this affects the future of children, young people, and the environment. It is so important to understand this because it is only when we see the real value of the missing energies, and what blocks them, that we can activate fully the *lower right* quadrant.

Only then, will we be able to galvanize into action the finer upper level feminine energy aspects, the *compassionate, loving and empathetic* qualities of higher brain awareness, and only by activating these missing precious human resources can we create more caring global cultures; those which protect the most vulnerable.

CHAPTER TWENTY-TWO

The invisible Energy Fields

"Goodbye," said the fox. "And now here is my secret a very simple secret: It is only with the heart that one can see rightly; what is essential is invisible to the naked eye."
Antoine de Saint-Exupery

As global citizens we grow up in very different cultures, but they are all similar in one respect, given that they have the power to define who we think we are. We grow to believe that we understand ourselves, or paradoxically, we do not even question who we are or how our minds work. We lose sight of the fullness of our own potential. The focus is now more about how we have integrated the energy and power which we accumulated through our childhood experiences, into the society we live in. This then becomes the position from which we relate to the world around us.

The tragedy is that by doing this, we overlook or suppress vital aspects of our own mind and consciousness. We are just not aware that there is so much more to each of us that we have never had the opportunity to explore or understand, which could impact greatly on our lives.

Christopher Chabris and Daniel Simons conducted and taped a simple experiment on human awareness factors with students in a psychology course they were teaching at Harvard University. They explain how people go through life thinking they know how their minds work and why they behave the way they do, when in fact many of us, have no clue.

In their book *The Invisible Gorilla,* Chabris and Simon explain six everyday illusions that profoundly influence us and impact on our lives. They are illusions of attention, memory, confidence, knowledge, cause and potential, and how the distorted beliefs held about these matters are not just wrong, but wrong in dangerous ways.

The experiment consisted of two basketball teams, one dressed in black shirts and one in white. Their task was to count the number of times they passed the ball. Meanwhile, halfway through the game another student dressed in a gorilla suit walked amongst the players, thumping her chest for nine seconds then walked off.

After the game the players were asked if they had noticed anything unusual. Had they noticed anyone other than the players? Did they see a gorilla?

Incredibly, about half the students were shocked that they had not noticed anything unusual; they had not seen a gorilla!

They did not miss the gorilla because of eye problems or physical blindness, but because of 'in-attentional blindness'. Their attention was so totally focused on the ball and counting their passes no room was left to pursue a wider perception of events. In this instance it was not so much about their upbringing or social conditioning as to why they did not see the gorilla, it was more about how their attention was focused on counting the passes they made. So what's wrong with that you might ask?

Interestingly, there is nothing wrong with that when you are playing basketball but it's a different matter if you are doing something potentially life threatening, such as driving a car while talking on a mobile phone, where lack of attention could lead to an accident.

But a clear and demanding focus was not the main reason Chabris and Simon wrote their book. They wrote it because they were more surprised by the student's reactions to the results of the test when it was pointed out to them. They found it difficult to believe they had missed seeing the gorilla. Some said "I missed that!", "No way!" One man who was tested later by *Dateline NBC* for their report on this research said, "I *know* that gorilla didn't come through there the first time". Other subjects accused the authors of changing the tapes while they weren't looking. They wrote it because they were more surprised by the student's reactions to the results of the test when it was pointed out to them.

The experiment illustrates most of all the powerful and pervasive influence of the *illusion of attention,* during which we experience far less of our visual world than we think we do, as those basketball students showed. Their attention was so focused that they missed seeing the gorilla. In the same way, our focus on safety slips when driving while talking on a mobile phone as we become so caught up in conversation that we don't see another car coming at us. Although this may seem a simple, logical fact, it is surprising how difficult it is for many to comprehend. Those things we don't see when our mind is occupied by other events mask a 'striking mental blindness' that many people refuse to recognize. Such events are called 'everyday illusions' because we know these beliefs and intuitions are flawed, that something in this picture is not right, but the illusion stubbornly persists.

While the authors' experiments reveal unexpected insights, they also highlight a faulty view of the world around them, shared by many. They have written critically about issues similar to my own in regard to alternative perspectives within our universe. However, in view of their study and research, what is most *amazing to me*, is that they do not support the idea of 'other realities'.

CHAPTER TWENTY-THREE

The Trouble with Harvard

"Only those who will risk going too far can possibly find out how far one can go." T. S. Elliot

In *The Rider Encyclopaedia* of *Eastern Philosophy and Religion*, viewpoints on *Buddhism & Taoism* compiled by respected writers on these subjects, state in the introduction that "Wisdom" is meant here primarily in the Buddhist sense of *prajna*: that is, not as mere intellectual achievement but rather as personally immediately experienced intuitive wisdom, the essence of which is insight into the true nature of the world as well as eschatological matters. So we are not dealing with an accumulation of factual knowledge in the form of objective dates and measurements as in natural science in the Western sense. This is true even though the research methods of Eastern religion are no less pragmatic than those of Western science. In fact their results have shown incomparably greater coherence and stability over millennia and across all cultures than the lasting "facts" of the natural sciences: however, the essence of the *insights* gained through their methods, as all wisdom teaching repeatedly stresses, cannot be conveyed in a conceptual, rational manner."

They explain how one does not need detailed chemical analysis of a pear to understand the experience of biting into a pear. Only someone who has had the experience of eating a pear is in a position to use these concepts with *real knowledge of their meaning.*

Knowledge is conveyed through direct experience as explained by associate research professor of the Neuroscience Research Center at the University of Montreal, Mario Beauregard, PH.D., who in his book *Brain Wars*, says, "Very often, perhaps more often than you think, ordinary people have unexplained experiences that defy the boundaries and expectations of traditional science."

Beauregard cites case after case of these experiences which led him to explore these phenomena more deeply. He cites the case study of London cabbies by Dr. Eleanor Maquire from London's University College who conducted magnetic resonance imaging (MRI) brain scans on sixteen cabbies. The findings showed how the extensive training they went through to remember their driving areas actually increased the size of their brains. So we are not confined to the 'brains we are born with', because the adult human brain "is always changing its structure and function by creating new neuron and synaptic connections, and reorganizing existing neuronal networks."

Did they discover God exists? "No, but they can and did demonstrate that the mystical state of consciousness really exists, which is not such a simplistic explanation as many 'materialists' who think that the distinction made between the mind as an immaterial entity and the brain as a bodily organ have no real base". Many materialists explain these experiences as merely a "God gene", God spot" or a "Switch in the brain".

In an attempt to disprove the mystical experiences of *The Secret* and its founder Rhonda Byrne, in a *New York Times* article *Fight 'The Power,* September 24, 2010, materialists Chablis and Simons continue their theme as they discard 'non-proven' theorists such as Byrne with a little sophistry, saying that "the onslaught of pseudoscientific jargon serves mostly to establish an "illusion of knowledge," as social scientists call our tendency to believe we understand something much better than we really do. In one clever experiment by the psychologist Rebecca Lawson, people who claimed to have a good understanding of how bicycles work (and who ride them every day) proved unable to draw the chain and pedals in the correct location."

No matter how or if we differ in our views, do *non-proven theorists* such as Rhonda Byrne, or you and I, need to completely understand the physics of the universe, or the detailed chemical analysis of a pear, or draw the workings of a bike, to understand their essence? No. And just like scientists, our experiences or results may differ, but there is an underlying theme constant throughout all non-theorists experiences, which is that an unlimited, and yet equally valid range of experiences and knowledge exists beyond the physical world; and science cannot prove such insights to be false or invalid.

In fact there are many scientific studies which prove that same knowledge to be real; Beauregard explains further when he with Denyse O'Leary went on to write, *The Spiritual Brain: A Neuroscientists Case for the Existence of the Soul.* After recording the experiences of Carmelite nuns at the Universite de Montreal, one of the nuns described *uno mystica* saying "I don't know how much time passed. It is like a treasure, and intimacy. It is very, very personal. It was in the centre of my being, but even deeper. It was a feeling of fullness, fullness, fullness."

Along with doctoral student Vincent Paquatte, Beauregard first had to convince the nuns they were sincere; that they understood there was a world beyond matter and physical phenomenon. They explained they were not materialists in that sense: they did not doubt in principle that a contemplative might contact a reality outside herself during a mystical experience. Beauregard stated that he "went into Neuroscience in part because, "I knew experimentally that such things can indeed happen."

Is it the materialist doctrine, whether it is education, science, or business - or the underlying concepts within them – that are the real myths haunting the world today? Is it as Larry Dossey, author of *Reinventing Medicine* explains, "The current assumption that the brain makes consciousness, like the liver makes bile, and that human consciousness is confined to the brain and body, can only be called neuromythology".

Could it be the opposite as the cabbie experiment explains where consciousness is reshaping the brain?

Is 'the trouble with Harvard', and many other great traditional halls of learning, that they are not open to the thought that *things can happen*. They are not tracking knowledge itself per se, but are merely expanding on literal evidence within the limited paradigms of academia and good scholarship, where there is little scope for reshaping the Western thought system; the fixed mind that continues to conceptualize and compartmentalize life solely through left brain, physical theory?

CHAPTER TWENTY-FOUR

The Elephant in the Room

"Education's purpose is to replace an empty mind with an open one." Malcom Forbes

Why do researchers like Christopher Chabris and Daniel Simons who study the nature of the mind, and witness the impact that these illusions have in their own lives, continue to have misgivings of life beyond the prevailing brain-mind paradigm. For instance, why is it safer in some places for cyclist on the road? They found it is safer on the roads when car drivers *expect,* and therefore look out and allow for cyclists to occupy the same space. They continue to call these behaviors everyday illusions. However, while their theory has been relevant and repeated successfully in many more experiments because they affect our behavior literally every day, the authors themselves do not expect or deem it to be relevant to pursue this knowledge, outside of their own physical realm.

We know money exists so why do some people make money while others do not? How is it that some people can be likened to entrepreneurs; keen to find potentially rewarding prospects. Why? Because they think creatively, are prepared to take risks and find business opportunities where most people do not. They look for the unexpected, whereas most of our young people are educated into conformity which discourages looking 'outside the box.' It is like the energy field paradigm we live in where many energy field traits remain largely unseen because their existence is not registered in their consciousness.

Without that knowledge or those insights which are neither expected nor valued within the literal Western mind, we lose out, not only in achieving greater scientific knowledge, but also financial and health benefits for communities and relationships; all those areas which have been compartmentalized, and which when merged would improve the quality of our lives greatly.

Isn't life far too complex to stop here, to relegate the whole universe solely to what can be physically proven? To only one area of human consciousness, especially when it is staring the authors in the face and they are actually describing and writing about it?

And remember Chabri and Simon's words, "They wrote the book because they were most surprised by the student's reactions to the results of the test when it was pointed out to them. They found it difficult to believe that they had missed seeing the gorilla. "I missed that!", "No way!", "I *know* that gorilla didn't come through there the first time". Other subjects accused the authors of changing the tapes while they weren't looking." It appears the authors *know* that alternative realities do not exist either.

To quote *The Invisible Gorilla* further, "Much of our memory for the world can be distorted to match our conceptions of what we should remember, and just as we can fail to see the gorilla around us, because they do not fit with our preexisting expectations, our understanding of our world is systematically biased to perceive meaning rather than coincidence. And we are usually unaware of these biases, and almost any quality can be measured well enough to be studied scientifically"

How aware are Christopher Chabris and Daniel Simons of their own bias? Why aren't they taking their research further to study the vast unknowns of the intangible mind? Why do they act as many scholars do when they hit the wall, the edge of their educational paradigm; they start to stigmatize and ridicule the ideas and insights that they fail to understand, those they cannot comprehend? Why? Because similar to the basketball-players in the gorilla experiment who refused to believe what was pointed out to them, even when shown the filmed and recorded evidence, they refuse to. They simply continue to defend and justify their flawed beliefs.

And it is here that everyday illusions reach even larger and more terrifying levels of application, where it is not so much about the gorilla in the room, but the elephant in the room of finance, education and science; where many financial advisors, academics, politicians and research "experts", are renowned for over-riding public opinion while creating community "health and safety" policies, that are not inclusive of all evidence.

CHAPTER TWENTY-FIVE

Ending Compartmentalized Energy Field Patterns

"To realize that you do not understand is a virtue; not to realize that you do not understand is a defeat." Lao Tzu

MEN: Are they the biggest problem in the world? explains how we have come to expect, or not to expect certain outcomes or results, because we have learned to deny parts of ourselves. Our expectations then affect how men and women, unconsciously measure their place and worth in the world around them. The fact that some energy field traits are unknown or lost to the conscious mind doesn't mean they are not there. It just means they are not seen or acknowledged by us, and in the modern era where we have to adhere to pre-ordained environments, these differences have become more submerged and their effects more subtle. Those who suffer from both gender and cultural attentional blindness, do not see and value the intangible qualities of compassion, empathy, divine love, nurturing, and passivity. As explained in MEN, what is not seen by the worlds of business and science, is therefore not financially valued, acknowledged or rewarded.

Innocence	**Compassion**
Curiosity	**Protector**
Inspiration	**Divine Love**
Mercy	**Empathy**

Active	**Nurturing**
Masculine	**Feminine**
Logical	**Intuitive**
Competitive	**Passive**
Independent	**Interdependent**
Closed	**Transparent**
Hierarchical	**Inclusive**

Illustration 5

How do we move forward in a world where people refuse to acknowledge many gentle and vulnerable aspects of their own being, and will not entertain the idea of a greater more conscious reality? Whether we find our experiences easy or difficult, based on scarcity or abundance, it is likely we will see the world through those eyes. We see the world not as it is, but as we are conditioned to believe it is. Where not only do we miss out personally, but culturally and scientifically on a great deal of knowledge, we miss small acts of love and kindness that connect the heart and mind, and have the potential to free many from relentless and erroneous beliefs, where whole cultures could disengage from wars that have endured for a thousand years and continue on through stubborn gender, ethnic and social codes.

These same traits blindly manifest to dominate the more gentle human qualities not only in capitalist systems, but also to a large degree have plundered human consciousness for the last two millennia.

However if Capitalism and Free Trade were any different with their foundations in free market Bull enterprises, which are being touted as such an improvement over Communism or Socialism, then why is it still only working for 1% of the global population? Why does such a small portion of humanity benefit from such an abundance of global wealth? Why isn't the system working for everybody?

What does a compartmentalization of energy field traits mean for men and women who are undergoing the difficulties of financial imbalance throughout their community, with ongoing and entrenched beliefs of entitlement? Furthermore does an imbalance of power and corruption now only occur in Capitalist or Free Trade environments?

I didn't really question in any depth the implication of ethnic or social conspiracy theories, gender, corruption or otherwise so much when writing 'MEN' or how they impact on the global financial crisis, but I do now: If you earn a living, have a credit card or borrow money for anything at all to do with finance, then you need to understand how the foundation of credit and the impact of global monetary policy affects every aspect of your life.

What is more, by continuing with old world gender, and cultural dogmas and hatreds, which allow little movement for the interconnection of life-force, how would the more elusive human elements arise? How could change be made that would effect a more equitable financial system for 99% of all people. And without a connected financial life-force how can global consciousness expand if free reign is still blocked by the financial speculators, the fiscal dominators and the human controllers, who left to their own devices will continue suppressing vital human life-force and energy resources, as they grab the bulk of the world's wealth for themselves?

CHAPTER TWENTY-SIX

The Banking System

"I believe the banking institutions are more dangerous to our liberties than standing armies."
Thomas Jefferson

Christopher Houghton Budd in an interview with Chico Aoki, a specialist in the study of central banks, the evolution of the economy, and fair pricing says "What is critical about this is to distinguish between the function of a central bank in banking terms, about what is called free banking, and what happens to a central bank when it becomes a state agency."

He explains how we need to get back to when there were no central banks by name. For example "the Bank of England was not initially a central bank. There was no idea of a central bank at that time, in the 17th century. In particular, the Bank of England's origin was a fight with the King because the King used the resources of the country to finance his wars ... Charles I had done this and he did not pay it back so he was executed. Then his son Charles II did a similar thing. The third time, when William III wanted to borrow money the bankers said, 'This time we'll make a contract. We will lend you 1.2 million pounds at 8% forever in exchange for a contract to have a monopoly and the name 'Bank of England'...it was a clever marketing trick. By using the name Bank of England, a monopoly was created, even if there's not a monopoly option in law. Herein also lie the origins of national debt.

Other banks in other countries created the same arrangement with their governments. In terms of their relationship to other banks this was what we call today a competitive market. In order to become what we call a central bank, it was necessary to undertake functions that became common practice, common to all banks... The Bank of England, as a private institution became the 'clearing bank' for all the banks, the bank in the middle of all the banks. This is why technically it came to be called a central bank because all the banks cleared through the bank in the middle. It is a clearing house... the bank in the middle of the system

Christopher Houghton Budd says: The question is not how one powerful country (now the USA) can unite the world economy in its own interest, but how all the countries of the world independently work together to create a world economy. So you don't follow the light of only one of them. Leonard Cohen understands this: "Democracy is coming to the USA." ... It has to be something that people genuinely recognize, not something the US reinforces with its army or with the tricks it plays with the Chinese economy: passing dollars through China and pretending that China has all America's dollars... American income will come into the wrong relationship to its debt and this will crash the dollar. In fact the dollar has already crashed because the loss of its AAA rating constitutes a complete crash of the dollar. ... On arriving at this point in history, the rest of the economy will suffer.

And how does the impoverished world economy rebuild itself? I don't see poor countries made poor by their own lack of effort, I see countries made poor because of foreign policy ... All that really happened was that the imperial powers said to their colonies "now you can be non-colonies, that means your market will not be yours, nor will your resources: they'll stay with us ... Columbia was a colony of the US when looked at in terms of its economic relationships. It had to export its coffee at the price determined by the US, but they said, "Not anymore. That is not the true price. We will now sell the coffee at a price that is real for us in Colombia".

It was not only Columbia. Friedman's Free Trade policies devastated countries like Argentina and Chile, where brutal pressures were used to force populations into financial hardship.

"This event is lost in the heartbreaking history of Columbia. Responsibility for the lost destiny of Colombia must be laid at the feet of the narcotic trade. The idea that Colombia would eventually state that, "from now on we sell our coffee at the price that benefits us," could not have been foreseen. So, looking at Colombia as the first case of a country, 'taking the bull by the horns, a true price for their coffee was arrived at. A true or correct price is one that both parties can profit from, not just one party.

We, as citizens of this country need to control our own economy by incorporating three components:

1. Be able to discuss price, not be told the price of our commodities

2. Issue our own money

3. Create our own credit

This means we don't need the IMF or the World Bank.

It is not possible to continue with a world economy that is created and controlled by one country, the US, which sets the price, issues the US dollar to the world and controls credit creation through Wall Street. Technically it is not possible to continue on in the old ways... the citizens of every country have to create money, issue credit and name their prices. This will stabilize the dollar and over time the relationship between the country's income and its debt will become a healthy one."

It's all well and good to talk but how do you put these ideals into practice, so they will benefit everyone. And what about our hard earned money? Is it being invested in what is real growth for the future and the next generation? Will our purchasing power contribute toward the wealth and growth of the global population's economy, and how do we achieve accountability by businesses to support the health of the environment and the planet?

Prevailing systems serve to strengthen the growth of criminal systems, both legal and illegal. These unsanctioned and self-replacing programs have been activated to corrupt infiltrate and disable the majority of the world's inhabitants by crippling their ability to earn a living wage while caring for their family and their environment. These are the end results of a globally insidious dysfunctional power structure which has been inflicted on our civilization.

Answers to many of the present global problems can be found by researching, developing and activating technology within a whole brain energy system, one within a new financial consciousness which expands the growth and wellbeing of all traits within the individual energy field, leading to the health and wellbeing of the whole environment. Through more inclusive, workable social and financial systems, the wider village, town or country is embraced by systems that first and foremost enable the individual to grow and prosper. And the question is what would happen to the consciousness of the planet if the whole energy field spectrum were to be established?

CHAPTER TWENTY-SEVEN

RealStew: A Healthy Disregard for the Impossible

"What I've come to learn is that the world is never saved in grand messianic gestures, but in the simple accumulation of gentle, soft almost invisible acts of compassion."
Chris Abani

When the Energy Field Structure is applied to healing an individual, it brings conscious*ness* to the body, mind and spirit to instigate self-healing. Similarly, when the missing gender and cultural traits are acknowledged personally and activated globally they merge and manifest on a global scale, through the interconnection of consciousness. This also shows in the wider range of social interaction those traits which are missing; how each can be reduced or on the contrary, what can be increased when it is needed for each society to function in more effective and healthy ways.

It is said that the one constant in life is change but change at this level is more than just a change of mind, it requires a change of heart, of our perception of the world. To acknowledge that what seems like the permanent and unmovable must now move and that there are ways to accomplish this.

The energy field structure demonstrates how the global business process, like the economy or personal reality, is not a fixed or permanent form to which we are chained forever. But it does have basic guiding principles. It shows how a new and interconnected financial structure is essential and also workable.

Energy Fields demonstrate how an interactive business system works most effectively when based on an expression of humanity's merging and flowing interactive energetic principles; by bringing the invisible into being. In this way a whole new, more balanced, more equitable financial model for the community can and has emerged - and this is what makes the RealStew model different from the rest, and why it works where so many others have failed.

RealStew's aims comply fully with the variable ideals inherent in whole Energy Field principles; through the connection and interaction of interconnecting energy field traits. This creates an easy flow of communication within structures which share values of equality with male and female, physical and spiritual energies interacting consciously. Where different traits are more visible and in motion at different times dependent on the circumstance.

Innocence	**Compassion**
Curiosity	**Protector**
Inspiration	**Divine Love**
Mercy	**Empathy**

Active	**Nurturing**
Masculine	**Feminine**
Logical	**Intuitive**
Competitive	Passive
Independent	Interdependent
Closed	**Transparent**
Hierarchical	**Inclusive**

Illustration 6

As described in the Butterfly Effect in chaos theory, small changes to the energy field of one person, or one aspect of an energy field, can bring unforeseen enhancement to the system. The flapping of small wings represents a small change in the initial conditions, which cause a series of events that lead to large-scale alterations of results. Therefore, what appears at first to be as insignificant as a bee in Mr Ingram's hives, or chaos in a business environment, can in fact be masking great happenings for the local environment, which grow to effect the whole planet. It means that even the most tender, inspirational ideas that are floating in our minds are able to flourish and grow in systems founded on any combination of the following principles:

- Independent *while nurturing*
- Active *while inclusive*
- Competitive *while inspirational*
- Transparent *while hierarchical*
- Closed *while merciful*
- Compassionate *while independent*
- Male *aligned with female*
- Earth *aligned with spirit or*
- Passive aligned *with Divine Love*

With this in mind, is it time to evaluate your own situation and check out where you think humanity perceives its future? Where are we right now? And where do we want to go? Ask some questions about the problems you are currently facing. Ask yourself "What do I most value?" Then decide, "What is the best way forward to improve my own financial position?"

Change and progress are seldom initiated from the top or by succumbing to old rules. They are more likely to begin out on the periphery; supported and nurtured by individuals who not only see the need for change, but like Paddy have the courage and commitment to draw together the forces they need to activate progress within the system.

New technologies have altered the relationship we have with our own money into models that have worked for the benefit of banks, utility suppliers, communications, social and business systems and those who now control how we shop and spend. However, what we once regarded as unmoveable institutions are having to move. To quote Paddy Delaney we must have 'a healthy disregard for the impossible'

Instead of treading the same threadbare, narrow path of well worn, unworkable and dominating financial systems thousands of people are considering the RealStew alternative, a concept to turn their own vision into reality by making space for curiosity and inspiration to blossom in their lives and community

Ask yourself if you want to continue with the global devastation that is being caused right now by the progenitors of old world belief systems that cloud the present economy creating hardship and despair for whole communities. Or do you want your voice to be heard, by being part of a movement creating change by rebuilding global consciousness through inspirational economic means, based on sound whole energy field principles?

As old financial structures are overturned, it's time to start preparing for a new era where dreams and visions can come forward to find the fertile ground of a wholly conscious structure, able to nourish the more tender and delicate aspect of the soul.

Depleting energy from vulnerable sectors cannot continue feeding the gluttonous habits of one limited system, but every person making small changes will help to bring about bigger changes, until eventually, they become part of a connected system of sharing communally generated wealth, based on the theory of six degrees of separation.

Creating a new economy requires a different measure for sharing wealth by introducing a just and workable personal consciousness; where we are in our own way contributing to the Butterfly Effect by creating a momentum of abundance globally.

CHAPTER TWENTY-EIGHT

Are they a Bunch of Delusional Dreamers?

"I really didn't foresee the Internet. But then, neither did the computer industry. Not that that tells us very much, of course – the computer industry didn't even foresee that the century was going to end." Douglas Adams

The RealStew Way brings real alternatives where other systems like Communism and Socialism which tried to equalize wealth simply made all people poor and deleted their inspiration: systems such as rampant Capitalism have also proved to be too limited in their ideals of human values. What is wealth? What makes a functioning society wealthy in emotional, mental and spiritual values? Capitalism, like Communism and Socialism, has overlooked important human traits when assessing their systems of wealth distribution.

The old forces dominant in the 20th Century brought about horrendous misery to millions of men, women and children, and all change was based on the old power system of control, competition, independence and hierarchy; where people were refused information and transparency, as is occurring now with corporations and governments bid to control the internet, thus keeping people in states of grinding poverty, denying them the chance to expand their awareness or gain an inflow of new knowledge which can be shared and communicated to others. There has been:

- Action ... *without compassion*
- Competitiveness ... *without empathy*
- Independence ... *without interaction*
- Hierarchical ... *without nurturing*
- Closed ... *without transparency and inclusiveness*

We were born in exciting times, where the need for a profound shift in human consciousness has landed on our doorstep. Where it is not only possible, but it is essential for us to expand our minds and activate whole brain thinking; including that side of the brain, the upper right side, which has so often, and for so long been seen as the work of the devil, where the controllers of hearts and minds suppressed populations from experiencing and expressing their more intangible, transformative powers.

Besides, when compassion, empathy and love are limited by various versions of a separate and virtual ideal spiritual achievement, it is nearly impossible to attain characteristics which most women, and certainly few men, would want or could ever achieve on earth; it reduces those connecting to female traits, as inferior.

Innocence	**Compassion**
Curiosity	**Protector**
Inspiration	**Divine Love**
Mercy	**Empathy**
Active	Nurturing
Masculine	Feminine
Logical	Intuitive
Competitive	Passive
Independent	Interdependent
Closed	Transparent
Hierarchical	Inclusive

Illustration 7

Whether we are male or female, the life-force of left and right, upper and lower brain activity illuminate the richer dimensions of possibilities within us. When they balance and combine, their energy moves us closer to achieving our greatest and unknown potential. Each diagram shows areas we can work with, that raise us above the merely mundane and take us to supposedly impossible realms; beyond the separation of our roles as the male and female personality programming we are familiar with and have been conditioned to. When we enter these higher realms we begin to realise the unlimited nature of our hearts and minds.

The characteristics of *compassion, empathy and divine love*, are not merely for divinely guided other realms, they are part of our visible living environment. Where direct intention manifests itself as electric – magnetic energy to change the molecular structure of matter. By including these traits in our personal and working lives, we bring to the world their gifts while actualizing a new consciousness for humanity.

The old and the new with all their energetic characteristics nurtures change in the hearts and minds, while feeding all aspects of the right and the left brain energies, strengthening our life-force and revitalising the structure of the planet.

Through the invigorated and interconnected system, new life-force and its feminine energy field traits are available to support the finest aspects of human consciousness, which in turn activates the actions we take to empower, or care, for those who are weakest, or most vulnerable in society. This allows whole working systems to activate and maintain the health and wealth of a wholly inspired humanity:

- People capture the nature and eternal spirit of their essential inspirational energies, personally activating them communally and globally
- Through this, people take back ownership of business systems

- People replace faceless corporate behemoths that presently rule the globe

It means companies like RealStew who work to bring a new system to fruition, are holding a space for growing communities to bring forth the unknown. They bring an antidote to indifferent global finances, and the cruel, indiscriminate, unbridled greed of Wall Street Markets that decimate the hopes and dreams of young people and make it impossible for the elderly to retire with wealth and security. We as participants are able to poke the Bull in the eye by revitalizing a crooked-thinking system, replacing it with a workable business model where those young people currently roaming the streets unemployed and purposeless, become active and aware participants in their communities as they plan their own economic lives.

In a universe consisting of opposing, yet not mutually exclusive forces, does each perspective of the material and intangible views, of left and right brain understanding, have their own intrinsic value to humanity? Does the truth lie within each of us, and do we by expanding our knowledge as Neuroscientist Mario Beauregard has done, find new frontiers are opening, and by delving into the unknown consciousness of the collective mind are we merging the information science has provided, while at the same time exploring the answers life gives us through direct experience? The future is the space where knowledge is being experienced as real, not conceptualized and compartmentalized. We are entering the new age of *Wisdom Teachings.*

CHAPTER TWENTY-NINE

The Basis of a New World Economy

"Every time you spend money you are casting a vote for the kind of world you want." Anna Lappe

Christopher Houghton Budd goes further: "I would approach this crisis in an unusual, unexpected way. What phenomena are all happening at the same time? One is: The income of the US and the debt of the US are in a wrong relationship. That means finally the US cannot be the world currency.

All the attempts made since 1971 to avoid this problem now no longer work. You can't hide this problem anymore. And I would be looking at what else is happening at the same time. And I would point immediately to two phenomena. If you don't find a basis of a new world currency, the economy will become militarized. It would be kept as it is by military and police forces. This is what we call the Iraq war.

Then there is the second phenomenon: graduates without a future, the Facebook generation. You can see the Facebook generation saying it has no future, and it is not a political statement, it's existential. The markets have come out of the subprime because the government bought their toxic debt. They got their money out and went into the commodities market. Now they buy all the world food and they sell it at a higher price five minutes later... You must not make it impossible for people to buy bread. This is a huge phenomenon today that is driving most of today's problems. The financial crises have now become a real economic crisis, and young people are saying: "We have no future and no food." Sending the army in or the police will not solve this.

You will find that the young people, whether they are in Somalia, or India or Brazil, they all have the same kind of gesture: "I need a career. I need a job. I need to be capitalized for what I want to do and not for what you want me to do, because you guys have no jobs left. And I need to buy food to eat so I can do what I want to do."

Christopher Houghton Budd goes on to describe how he would replace the dollar as the world currency, "...but we need to look at young people in every country and we need to base the cover of the money in that country on the services or the goods they provide for other people. And the basis for credit in those countries is: you invest in the initiative of these young people. So if a young person says, "I want to open a restaurant," this is the foundation of money. If people want to eat in this restaurant, they will pay money. So by being a restaurateur he/she emits money, not the central bank. When he/she says, "Please lend me the capital to open my restaurant," this is the basis of credit. It is not created by the central bank or the markets: it is created when we lend money to young people *without* collateral. So for example if you issue a youth bond, this will have huge consequences in the countries where young people see no future.

So you don't start by saying, "What do we do with young people?" You have to ask them, "What do you want to do with your life and how do we capitalize what it is that you want to do?" Then young people all around the world will show you what the next economy is …. Whereas, what we can say today is that the financial markets – that is to say agencies: pension funds and organizations, not actual people – have cornered the market in credit. And in every market, when you corner the market, you crash the market. So all these agencies, all the pension funds are institutions, not people. They have taken all the credit to themselves. In any market when you acquire everything you then crash the market."

Similar to this view, the best Bull investments will be those driven not by old financial markets, but by the inspirations of young people, those at the bottom of the financial heap, as they align their emerging awareness into meeting their own and other's needs. Where each country grows in its power as business is inspired by an emerging population. Where the community continues to nurture and stay connected to its young, through their growing spirit and ability to express their intelligence and inspiration, by bringing their ideas to fruition through pragmatic action, therefore giving them, and indeed all of us, more financial and personal freedom.

"So there is only one solution" continues Christopher Houghton Budd, "you extend credit to actual people, not institutions, who have a life in front of them, who are full of enthusiasm, skills and talent and you ask them: "What do you want to do in service to your fellow man, and how do we capitalize your initiative?" You then create a new bond, a bond that is money lent only to young people on condition that they are not collateralized. The collateral is that you help them to achieve their intentions. You have no interest in real estate".

RealStew is similar in this way; it is in effect a Bull market: it sells shares and its business is the sale of technology and communication; its purpose is to make a profit which goes back into the community. As we have seen, the difference between RealStew and most Bull market based businesses, is that its foundation is based on sustainable growth and by sharing the profit amongst its members, every person receives income, not only those who have invested in shares.

A butterfly going about its business in Brazil will still impact on the global arena; it is all connected because it's a business different from the general Wall Street Markets as it feeds corporate life-force back to the community in the form of personal connections and finance.

The RealStew Way is unique in that it distributes information and wealth through six degrees of separation, and the peer-to-peer network. Every user of the system can share in the corporate profit while going about their normal life or business, with the added incentive of being part of an innovative movement for global change. Nobody needs to be thrown into the prison system to provide food for a wounded, craving bull, or get lost in the maze of welfare queues, or dysfunctional systems which pretend they care.

The Bull in ancient cultures was a magnificent, potent and benevolent beast and RealStew is Poking the Bull in the Eye reminding it of its noble past, ready to assist it back to its former glory. By instigating more caring cultures, greater awareness is activated, where through a domino effect we are stimulating those more intangible qualities that were inherent in all of us at birth.

Together, the Butterfly and the Bull are revitalizing human energy field traits through individual and global financial expansion. When systems are bursting with fresh life and vitality, they are creating a perfect climate for the expansion of a new world planet consciousness.

Innocence	Compassion
Curiosity	Protector
Inspiration	Divine Love
Mercy	Empathy
Active	Nurturing
Masculine	Feminine
Logical	Intuitive
Competitive	Passive
Independent	Interdependent
Closed	Transparent
Hierarchical	Inclusive

Illustration 8

Who would have thought a butterfly and a bull would come together to create such happenings. Where the world can be turned upside down by bringing an actual polarity shift into financial reality. Instead of global wealth being sucked into and dominated by one sector of humanity while the majorities suffer, its financial life-force can flow into each quadrant supporting and nourishing inspirational and merciful communities.

In *The Tipping Point*, Malcom Gladwell says, "We need to prepare ourselves for the possibility that sometimes big changes follow from small events, and that sometimes these changes happen very quickly."

CHAPTER THIRTY

When You Enter the Magic the Magic Enters You

*"Magic Swirls... The technical name for this energy is
"variable electro-gravitational mutable subatomic force."
Which doesn't mean anything at all – confused scientists just
gave it an important name so as not to lose face. The usual
term is "wizidrical energy' or " The Crakel"."*
Jasper Fforde

Great change is occurring as we move to synchronize with each other and to the earth, where a change in our energy is now altering the environmental paradigms of Biology and Medicine. Understanding and controlling energy like Harry Potter may sound like childlike nonsense but the more we put these concepts into practice, the closer we come to unveiling the mastery of Einstein and the theory of relativity. Where Einstein established a connection between space and time, where matter and energy are two parts of the same coin, $E=MC^2$.

Brian Cox, in an interview with Elizabeth Cline for *Seed Magazine* about Cox and Jeff Forshaw's new book, *Why Does E=mc^2?* says, "Whenever I bring up the subject of Einstein to my friends who *aren't* physicists, I typically only get one of two responses. Either it's something like, "Oh, the science guy with the weird hair?" Or they say, "**Eee** equals **emm see squared**!"... But what does it actually mean, and what makes it so important that even people who don't know the first thing about matter, energy, or even algebra can recite it?

When Einstein discovered the equation, that energy was equal to mass times the speed of light squared, there were a lot of different possible *physical* meanings that it could have. Which one was right? Did it mean?

- That one could simply convert mass into energy, and energy back into mass?
- That energy—pure, massless energy— would be affected by gravity and would *cause* gravity just as mass does?
- That, because radioactive materials emitted energy, their mass was being destroyed?
- That, because the Sun was emitting energy, *its* mass was being converted into energy?

Remarkably, $E=mc^2$ means *all* of these things. What's more, $E=mc^2$ tells us how much mass it takes to make a certain amount of energy. The speed of light is a huge, huge quantity. Square it, and it's even bigger. What this tells us is that a small, insignificant amount of mass can generate an amount of energy so fantastic it's barely fathomable.... This is the very frontier of what we know and what we understand."

It is where our intentions matter greatly and affect our life-force. It is through our life-force that we are able to bring our deepest desires into being; a change in mass consciousness brought about by raising our energy affects the density of our gravitational fields and takes us beyond the sum of our parts.

We are able to take quantum leaps, and when enough of us reach this state of consciousness we change the life-force of the planet. This is the chaos theory in action. By gathering the life-force of human energy traits we can transform any energy field virus to make quantum leaps in consciousness.

"With the merging and balancing of male and female, earth and spiritual energies, a transformation takes place within the universe. The connection of these energies creates a cosmic tapestry that expands these components and takes them beyond the sum of their parts" Excerpt from '*The Structure of Energy Healing*'.

Paddy and Mandy Delaney have pooled their natural proclivities into practical resources, enabling others to sustain and bring to consciousness their dreams, and share them through the use of easily accessible leading edge technology. *The RealStew Way* is making its way into the global financial arena, by providing opportunities for each of us to explore the infinite possibilities of the universe; to access and bring alive the unbelievable and intangible, and for them to become a visible part of this changing arena.

Canadian John de Ruiter, founder of *The College of Integrated Philosophy*, describes a change in consciousness as "When you're being a different level within than yourself, there's an electro-magnetic field to that and you experience it in your body. If you're not being that level, you won't experience its field, so that level of your body and reality won't be real to you. Once you awaken to it, you realize that the electro-magnetic field is moving and pulling you, and it's your way into being that level. First you awaken to that level, you notice that level, then in noticing it and attuning to it you awaken to the electro-magnetics of it. As you respond to it, you're moving electro-magnetically in the same way. This is what enables you to be that level".

When this level is attained you are awakened to an inner source, which allows the genius of the universe to work through you for the collective benefit of the community. There is no need for friction, because individual and universal life-force is working together for the whole, allowing for cooperation on a grand and global scale. So it really matters what you do and what you think because by choosing to be in a kinder better world you are already entering the magic: and when you enter the magic the magic is entering you.

CHAPTER THIRTY-ONE

Take Inspired Action Now

Blanche: *I don't want realism*
Mitch: *Naw, I guess not.*
Blanche: *I'll tell you what I want. Magic!*
Tennessee Williams: *A Streetcar Named Desire*

The failures of other systems have occurred because they did not meet the needs of the individual in conscious environments, and were unaware of the need to stimulate and encourage personal aspirations.

Lack of knowledge and unintentional social blindness which stifled curiosity, has only served to divide and enforce centuries of warring cultures and create financial vacuums, where inequality drove the earth's assets into the hands of a victorious few. It divided the earth's population into the haves or the have-nots, and generated a gross misuse of its resources and people. We have reached a point in global awareness where we understand how such destruction affects the environment and brings such misery to habitats and people. We understand clearly that it is time to end the indiscriminate use of the social and natural environment, and to have greater regard for the consequences of business and political actions.

Thousands of books have been written about these fundamental problems. New political, religious and business ventures have risen to fix personal and global financial imbalances but soon regressed to their former infractions, relapsing into their old financial hierarchies and social inequalities. There have been few sustainable and lasting solutions.

Simply put, they are the same energy traits in power which have only changed form, growing from varying levels of intimidating monopolies to more intimidating monopolies, achieving little that would ease the financial burden of millions. Social and cultural difficulties have become worse, where social and financial inequality has been instrumental in driving conflict and enforcing Free Trade growth.

Through Energy Fields we can see the underlying patterns that turn many good theories bad. Why, where and how old human traits keep re-emerging, and how new and exciting systems can fall back into their original social patterns, when powerful extremes take over and quash those who question and who have new and inspirational ideas.

Single-minded competition as the ultimate in human endeavour is in reality a farce, an anathema that contradicts our deepest instinct of inquiry, cooperation and collective values.

Social change and the forming of new structures occur through the actions we take as individuals. Change depends on us not aligning with old energy field systems that squander vast human potential but instead, instigating innovative and inspirational endeavours.

We need to build financial networks which support ideas that provide real solutions which allow us to grow physically, emotionally, mentally and spiritually, while enhancing the wellbeing and prosperity of human and environmental needs. Ideally, we then begin to activate personal dreams and visions within pragmatic business structures.

CHAPTER THIRTY-TWO

I Have a Dream

"Life is like a game of cards. The hand you are dealt is determinism; the way you handle it is free will." Nehru

Life experience has taught us hard economic lessons, that hierarchy and dominance in business are not the ultimate traits that drive people to achieve great success or to take us forward into wealth and happiness. We understand the unconscious underlying wisdom of a collective world in which each species interacts in mutually beneficial, expanding and contracting situations - with bold yet considerate energy forces that are designed to ebb and flow, rise and fall so people and animals can adapt to their environments and where all traits are equally vital.

This does not mean we don't compete or that we are victims of any life situation, but we can wake up to our own power of co-creation within the exciting and dynamic forces of universal aliveness: To become active participants in the vibrant merging and changing formation of life while understanding that with freedom we gain responsibility which means we must take our dreaming seriously.

Then, by creating a system that supports them our dreams can be realized. By activating the energy fields of the feminine, we are bringing the qualities of nurturing, empathy and compassion, into the world of action, interdependence and logic.

If we do not do this, then the most vulnerable aspects of humanity's energy field structure: innocence, inspiration and mercy will float around in obscurity, to be consumed by harsh realist establishments, and everything remains the same as it has been since the advent of Greek mythology where the powerful ate their son's too. Do we, like Cronos and Zeus, continue consuming our young, their dreams, energy and life-force: feeding them into craving greedy Bull markets for the sake of a powerful few?

Or does it mean that while we may be back where we started, everything has changed. If we again enter into competitive, logical and active markets, we can choose a totally different set of values: we can include those values which embrace the cherishing and sharing of more invisible resources, where each quadrant supports the others to activate its life-force.

Just by understanding the workings of a unified energy field theory, have we already altered the awareness of the planet? Do we now need only to galvanise its life-force by merging the wisdom of ancient cultures and science to assist their fusing? Are we witnessing the birth of a new world by bringing forth exciting new discoveries through the most marvellous universe of all – the interaction of our heart and mind?

Innocence	*Compassion*
Curiosity	*Protector*
Inspiration	*Divine Love*
Mercy	*Empathy*
Active	*Nurturing*
Masculine	*Feminine*
Logical	*Intuitive*
Competitive	*Passive*
Independent	*Interdependent*
Closed	*Transparent*
Hierarchical	*Inclusive*

Illustration 9

"I have a dream" said Martin Luther King, and we too can activate our own dreams through the growth of humaneness within supportive social environments. What we do matters in the emerging awareness of a global system that is assisting in the manifestation of the unknown. As dreams become reality, we are released from complex social, political and financial turmoil, to be embraced within the finest traits of human dignity and wisdom.

And when life trips us up, we need only let go of the cloud of conditioning above our head that is the mirage, the hallucination of a Time conditioned heart and mind.

The Mayan calendar was correct and the world as we knew it has changed. By providing tools to access and bring alive the universal flow of consciousness humanity is awakening to a vibrant new world: one that allows for the realization of inspiration and the liberation of compassionate hearts and minds as they enter an entirely new business environment, that of a potent, yet benevolent Bull Market.

You may be a gentle listener or have a grand master plan, but each of us holds a space in time for competition, compassion and empathy to activate the joy of our wizidrical energy: You do not need to be a rocket scientist to understand these concepts, but simply choose through your own awareness, to merge or not with Life's forces.

Like the stillness of a chrysalis doing the job a caterpillar is destined to do, we are emerging, waking to our true purpose by harnessing the forces that transmute energy and matter, as mastered through the magnificent intelligence of the universe.

"This has never been done before," said Paddy, "but it's no good being on the right track and just sitting there. You must make yourself available for the next thing to happen, to take you to the next level; this is the nature of serendipity. It is a way of finding sustainable answers, the place where anything is possible. The universe gives you what you need and there is always something out there for you. There is no failure. There is only movement. Always. Expansion is occurring. Find reasons to say yes, or just do it. The modern pioneer is about embracing change and it is now up to us to explore, utilize and share a vast universe of untapped potential. It is about embracing technology, communication and resources while acting humanely. There are no extremes, whatever you do you do for the right reasons. With greater awareness of the human condition, you step out of the box and into a new world. Instead of living with the fear of failure, take inspired action. Do something that you are in all likelihood conditioned not to do".

Become part of a new way of looking at something that has always been there. Where people, not corporations take control of global resources; where competition is a healthy part of the system but at the end of the day, wealth generated within the co-operative and interconnected enterprise is shared with all those connected to it.

Knowing, happiness and wellbeing created through balanced energy field structures begin within us first then they spread ever outwards, transforming and influencing everything we do and everything we become. Each of us becomes that butterfly, touching down on the bull gently, paving the way for global change.

END

CONTACTS

www.pokingthebullintheeye@realstew.com
kayurlich@realstew.com
paddydelaney@realstew.com
www.pokingthebullintheeye@realstew.com/blog

Books by Kay Urlich

The Structure of Energy Healing
Soul Mate or Soul *In*mate? *Finding the Grail*
MEN: *Are they the Biggest Problem in the World?*

RealStew Nuts and Bolts

"Technology is destructive only in the hands of people who do not realize that they are one and the same process as the universe." Alan Watts

The World is changing, and YOU can be part of the Transition Team!

The RealStew Journey So Far

Up until recently a small New Zealand company, **RealStew Communications**, has stayed pretty much under the radar. It has been working away with plans to have a worldwide fully integrated communications system available from one single logged in environment.

Set up in 2009 (initially to raise funds for the Steiner School in Titirangi), the Founders ... Paddy Delany and a few family and friends dreamed of a company that had holistic ethics and values at its core. These included **transparency, economic and self-empowerment, sharing and abundance**. The Founders talked to others, and slowly the word spread and they drew to themselves people who care about such things, to become Foundation Members. From very small beginnings, a few people who believed this could be done, and just a couple of "IT" 'geeks' the vision grew.

However, the Founder's initial vision went way past the company's abilities to unfold, so it was slow at the beginning, then building by little steps for the next 3 or so years. During that time a lot of work was being put in behind the scenes, working on the millions of lines of code required for this ambitious project. The company started to build and provide FREE weblets (mini-websites) to anyone who wanted one. Each weblet had its own contact book and chat message ability. And, for just a small one off sum and $5 per month, it was possible to upgrade to a customized weblet with more 'business' orientation.

So far, the benefit of having a RealStew weblet has been the ability to communicate and engage with people's existing database of contacts. This communication has taken place whether both are members of RealStew or not. RealStew members have been accessing and using the platform for social / personal / business reasons, and this has not been dependent on them, or their contacts, belonging to any one particular service provider. This is a lot different to other platforms where, in general, everyone has to be on the same one to communicate.

With RealStew this is done seamlessly across all communication platforms, and in a way that enables members to be more proactive and responsive to the people that they communicate with, because they have a detailed history of that communication and the other's response. All documents, sent or received, are filed under the person's name for easy access, and therefore communication comes from a more informed position.

Many things changed for the company in December 2012 when it was accepted as "Executive in Residence" at the IceHouse, a business growth and incubator mentoring company that assists businesses to realize their potential. The IceHouse chooses companies that are based in New Zealand, have worldwide potential, has sound management, and executives with excellent business experience. IceHouse provides mentoring and access to experts in various fields that the business may not otherwise have been able to access. Since then much has been done by RealStew with the assistance of IceHouse mentors and other experts, all the while retaining the same ethics and values.

What does all this mean to you?

Whether you are an individual, business or organisation, all of the above is available to you now, as a RealStew member. You can choose to have a FREE weblet and contact book, or a personalized

/customized weblet. You also have, for just a small monthly fee, the ability to set up your own Blog. You can send a link to the blog to as many or as few of your contacts as you wish, providing them with information, updates, details of your services or products, etc. and with the ability to include photos or videos.

Being a member gives you access to all of this right now. And there is much more to come!   You will soon have the ability to write notes and set alerts to remind you when you next need to communicate with others. This is especially useful for those businesses where customers or clients book appointments to use your services. This allows you to be much more efficient in your 'filing' and communication.

It gets even more exciting! You will be able to access the (soon to be released) new business applications (apps) These will give you the ability to promote your products and/or services across the RealStew Platform via the affordable and integrated "**On-Line Shop**" and "**Created ads**" applications. This will be achieved in a way that will allow you to track every single viewing of your ads and clicks from new or existing customers wanting to find out more. When they do so, their contact details will be automatically added to your contact book so that continued communication with them can easily take place.

With the new apps you will also be able to promote all of your products or services. Plus for every single product or service in your business, create an individual QR (Quick Response) code which can be scanned by mobile, and then the product or service paid for via the

RealCoin gateway for which a mobile strategy is currently being developed.

RealCoin

The new digital Wallet!

- *"One new financial gateway that is good for everyone"*
- *"No transaction fees!"*
- *"No transactions reversed"*
- *"Micro transactions processed at nil cost"*
- *"Accredited Vendors and Buyers"*
- *"Merchant & Trade finance"*

Cash withdrawals via the PAYPAL gateway (In the future the plan is to install ATMs for cash withdrawal) or the accrued funds may be used to pay an account through the RealCoin gateway (with no transactional fees) for products and services offered by other RealStew members (and it is real money not points).

If a client wants to buy a big ticket item from you as a business member, the company has the ability and resources to offer to loan them the money (at 1% per annum) to pay for the purchase. This will be based on the history of that person's passive income from RealStew. (instead of keeping their money, as all the others do, RealStew shares it throughout the membership.) By participating in the program you will have the added advantage of having any online forms automatically populated at the time of purchase.

Research has shown that up to 25% of online shoppers abandon their order process due to frustration in filling in forms (Graphic Arts Monthly, 1999). As a merchant member you will have the ability to build your own loyalty programs and manage the issue, redemption and analysis of loyalty coupons through the same gateway. When the app goes live, the withdrawal will be done via the PAYPAL gateway or the accrued funds can be used to pay an account through the RealCoin gateway (with no transactional fees) for products and services rendered by other RealStew Users. This will be accessible through apps for mobile and tablets.

Each RealStew member will automatically have access to an online digital wallet. The holder of a digital wallet will be every user who has agreed to participate in the affiliate program. i.e. share in the revenue generated through the activity of people who are happy to use our apps (because they are affordable and effective).

When you, in your normal everyday communication with your database, create "links" and any number of those "links" decide to use one or more of our apps to increase the effectiveness of their communication, a portion of the recurring, generated fees received by RealStew are shared with you, as the initiating member, as a reward for your loyalty to the global sharing community. You are rewarded for your loyalty ... not for what you buy!

RealCoin Managing your finances has never been easier…

So now, with the RealStew platform, not only are you able to communicate more effectively and efficiently, you are also able to share in the rewards from doing so. You can also promote your products and/or services in a way that enables you to be more responsive, proactive and effective across all of your communications.

In summary, RealStew is a wonderful platform, built on a great set of ethics and values. The upcoming benefits to the members will be enormous. We really do care for and appreciate all the people who are coming into the RealStew space and setting the scene for a fairer, more communicative and abundant world.

The World Is changing… take the opportunity now to be part of the RealStew Transition Team!

Information correct as at 30/07/2013

Represents the **ripple effect** that RealStew can bring about with its unfolding in the social, cultural, and economic life of the whole.

 Represents the economic and self **empowerment** that RealStew can bring about, irrespective of any members current station in life.

 Represents the **abundance** that can unfold.

 Represents the **life-changing** impact that the RealStew movement can bring about.

 Represents the mantra of **sharing** that RealStew supports.

 Represents the transparency of RealStew processes.

 Represents the energy that will flow from Members working together.

 Represents the economic, cultural, and social wealth that RealStew can generate in the world.